Contract Law in the Slovak Republic

Contract Law in the Slovak Republic

Third Edition

Josef Fiala
Jan Hurdík
Katarína Kirstová

This book was originally published as a monograph in the International Encyclopaedia of Laws/Contracts.

Founding Editor: Roger Blanpain
General Editor: Frank Hendrickx
Volume Editor: Jacques Herbots

Wolters Kluwer

Published by:
Kluwer Law International B.V.
PO Box 316
2400 AH Alphen aan den Rijn
The Netherlands
Website: www.wolterskluwerlr.com

Sold and distributed in North, Central and South America by:
Wolters Kluwer Legal & Regulatory U.S.
7201 McKinney Circle
Frederick, MD 21704
United States of America
Email: customer.service@wolterskluwer.com

Sold and distributed in all other countries by:
Quadrant
Rockwood House
Haywards Heath
West Sussex
RH16 3DH
United Kingdom
Email: international-customerservice@wolterskluwer.com

Printed on acid-free paper

ISBN 97890-411-8742-0

e-Book: ISBN 97890-411-8765-9
web-PDF: ISBN 97890-411-8795-6

This title is available on www.kluwerlawonline.com

Printed and Bound by CPI Group (UK) Ltd, Croydon, CR0 4YY.

The Authors

Prof. JUDr. Josef Fiala, CSc. was born in Velké Meziříčí near Brno, Czech Republic, in 1953, and graduated from Faculty of Law, J. E. Purkyně University (now Masaryk University), Brno, in 1979, becoming a full-time lecturer in the same year and subsequently an associate professor (docent) in 1995. Since 2005, he has been a professor, and since 2003, he has also been lecturing at Palacký University, Olomouc. In addition to lecturing, research, and publication activities (as author or co-author he has published over thirty books and about 200 articles and papers in journals and specialized publications), he has been engaged in a number of other activities related to legal practice. In 1992, he was an assistant to a Justice of the Constitutional Court of the Czechoslovak Federative Republic; since 1995, he has been an assistant to a Justice of the Constitutional Court of the Czech Republic; in 1998–2002, he was a member of the civil law committee of the Legislative Board of the Government of the Czech Republic, and he is also a member of the Civil Code Re-codification Committee of the Ministry of Justice.

His dissertation on easement in 1984 brought him the degree of Candidate of Sciences (then an equivalent to Ph.D.), and in 1995, he gained a higher doctorate (docent) with the work 'Ownership of Flats in the Czech Republic'. Currently, he is the member of the Civil Law Department of the Faculty of Law, Masaryk University, in Brno. Since 2016, he is the Judge of Constitutional Court in Brno, Czech Republic.

The Authors

Prof. JUDr. Jan Hurdík, DrSc. was born in Třebíč, Czech Republic, in 1951, and graduated in 1976 from Faculty of Law, J.E. Purkyně University, Brno (now Masaryk University). He was a lecturer in the Department of History of State and Law in 1975–1976, an assistant and consequently a public prosecutor at the Public Prosecutor's Office in 1976–1980. In 1980 he became a member of the Civil Law Department of the Faculty of Law, Masaryk University, Brno, focusing mainly on civil law and private law jurisprudence as well as on civil procedure; and lecturing on civil law at Palacký University, Olomouc, at Bratislava School of Law (Slovak Republic). In 1984, he gained the degree of CSc. (then an equivalent to Ph.D.) for his dissertation 'Abuse of Civil Rights', and in 1995, he gained a higher doctorate (docent) with his work 'Problems of Law of Foundations and Endowments'. In 2001, he was awarded the scholarly degree of Doctor of Juristic Sciences (DrSc.) by the Czech Academy of Sciences in Prague for his work 'Legal Persons – General Legal Characteristics'. Since 2004, he has been a professor (graduated from University of Trnava, Slovak Republic). He is author or co-author of more than forty books and textbooks on various issues concerning civil law, and numerous articles and papers in specialized publications. In addition to that, he has been involved in a number of grant projects concerning university education in law, in various research projects, in the government committee preparatory work on the new Civil Code, and was the head of a legislative committee preparing the law on foundations and endowments. Currently, he is a head of the Civil Law Department of the Faculty of Law, Masaryk University, Brno. Since 2008 he has been a member of Acquis Group, since 2006 a member of SECOLA association, and since 2011 a fellow of European Law Institute.

The Authors

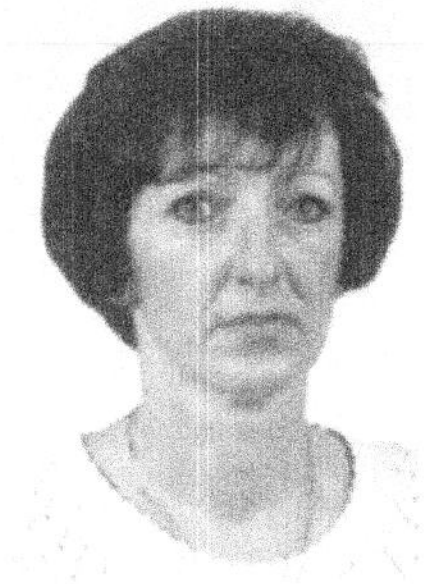

Doc. JUDr. Katarína Kirstová, CSc. was born in Košice, Slovak Republic, in 1950, and graduated from the Faculty of Law, Komenský University, Bratislava, in 1973. Since 1973, she has been a member of the Department of Civil Law, Faculty of Law, P.J. Šafařík University in Košice, first as an assistant and then as an assistant professor. In 1984, she defended her dissertation, 'Services in Civil Law', and was awarded her CSc. degree (Ph.D. nowadays). In 2001, she defended a habilitation dissertation on the topic 'Records of Immovable Assets from the Viewpoint of Rights' and was awarded the degree of docent (university lecturer). She is a co-author of textbooks, teaching aids in the area of civil law, and other papers published in law journals of the Slovak Republic. She is also an author of grant projects in the area of civil law. She is a member of the re-codification committee for the Civil Code attached to the Ministry of Justice of the Slovak Republic. The committee was charged with the task to work out the General Part of Contracts. At present, she is a member of the Department of Civil Law, Faculty of Law, P.J. Šafařík University in Košice.

The Authors

Table of Contents

Table of Contents

List of Abbreviations

al.	alinea (a clause within an article or within a § of a code or of a law see para.)
and fol.	and following (et sequentes, et sequential)
art.	article (section of a code or of a law – see §)
cf.	Compare
Col.	Collection of Legal Acts of the Slovak Republic
e.g.	exempli gratia (for example)
etc.	et cetera (and so on)
i.e.	id est (that is)
para.	paragraph (a clause within an article or within a § of a code or of a law – see al.)
§	paragraph (section of a code or of a law – see art.)
R	civil collection of rulings since 1.1.1993 published by the Supreme Court of the Slovak Republic
SR	Slovak Republic

List of Abbreviations

Preface

This book is a part of the encyclopaedia of law on contracts under the editorial project IEL, outlining the system of contract law in the Slovak Republic and reflecting the situation in the legislation by 1 February 2010. The work corresponds with the framework selected by the editor; however, it inevitably reacted to specific features of the law of contracts in the Slovak Republic, which made necessary the adjustment of some of the parts of the publication.

The current state of contract law in the Slovak Republic has several specific features that should be pointed out. First of all, the sources of (internal) contract law in the Slovak Republic are composed of two important acts: The Civil Code (Act No. 40, 1994 Col.) and Commercial Code (Act No. 513, 1991 Col.). Both Codes contain specific rules for both commercial and non-commercial contracts and deeds, but a strict dividing line between the two of them is often missing and thus, application of a particular rule of law to a given case is governed by rather complex rules.

Another feature influencing the character of the Slovak contract law is its dynamic development: following the 'Velvet Revolution' and the change of the political establishment after 1989, the law of contracts has, through a number of legislative changes including the Commercial Code re-codification, gradually returned to democratic standards of contract relationships, leaving aside the socialist experiment in law applied in the period from 1950–1989. However, a consistent change of the system of law makes it necessary to carry out an entire re-codification of private law as a whole, including the law of contract. Since 1992, legislative activities involving the entire re-codification of the Slovak private law have been in progress. The aim of the re-codification is a large new civil code, including family law. As for basic types of contracts, the new civil code should contain all standard contract types, including employment contracts and contracts used both in commercial relationships and beyond (which implies a 'commercialized' concept of the civil code). The code is also supposed to include the implemented European law of consumer protection.

Regarding the above-mentioned specific features of the transitional period of the Slovak contract law, the authors had to make some inevitable compromises with regard to standards of comparative contract law. These were brought about by the following circumstances in particular:

(1) A concise regulation of general provisions of contract law is in contrast to the detailed regulation of specific contract relationships in both the Civil and the Commercial Codes.
(2) The regulation of contract law is still different, to a large extent, from the standard, traditional forms of contract law and the modern projects of contract law.
(3) The conception, the content, and the terminology differences are quite apparent in individual contract relationships.

Due to the above-mentioned reasons, it was not possible to fully pattern the conception, the system, and the content of the Slovak contract law upon the standardized model structure of the monograph *Contract Law*, and the authors inevitably had to respect – in the interests of authenticity of the description of the Slovak contract law (which is not in the existing version legislatively harmonized and suffers from systemic imperfections) – these oddities, which may give an impression of incoherency and lack of a system. These oddities concern the terminology of the described institutes, too; the authors respect the special terminology of the Slovak contract law while at the same time striving to adapt it to the language standards of the 'European' English.

The authors would like to thank Mgr. Radek Šimek, Ph.D., Faculty of Law, Masaryk University, Brno, for the final language correction of the text.

This monograph has been written with the support of Czech Ministry of Education, Research Grant No. MSM0021622405.

General Introduction

§1. General Background of the Country

1. The Slovak Republic is a unitary state created after the splitting of Czechoslovakia on 1 January 1993. The Constitution of the Slovak Republic was adopted at the end of 1992, entering into force on 1 January 1993. The capital of the country is Bratislava. Since 1 May 2004, the Slovak Republic has been a Member State of the EU. The European law is in force in the Slovak territory, having supremacy over the Slovak law.

The legislative power is exercised by the Parliament of the Slovak Republic, which consists of the Chamber of Deputies (National Council) only. One hundred and fifty members of the Chamber of Deputies are elected in general, and direct elections are held every four years. Besides its legislative power, the Parliament also has other important functions. The Chamber of Deputies must pass the annual state budget and the final account. The National Council nominates a twofold number of candidates for judges of the Constitutional Court of the Slovak Republic, out of whom the President then appoints the respective number of judges. The President is elected by citizens in a direct election for five years. The same person may only be elected President for two consecutive terms at the most.

The executive power is partially vested in the Government of the Slovak Republic and partially in the President of the Slovak Republic, so he is also part of the executive power. He appoints the Prime Minister according to the result of the election to the Chamber of Deputies and appoints and dismisses each Minister of the Government on the proposal of the Prime Minister. The primary task of the Government consists in issuing regulations and making decisions needed for implementation of laws.

The judiciary power is independent of the executive and legislative powers. The Constitutional Court has the authority to pass judgments on constitutionality of laws enacted by the legislature and on regulations enacted by the executive authorities. The ordinary law courts are organized in three *levels* – district courts, regional or municipal courts, and the Supreme Court. Administrative justice is exercised by general courts; they have jurisdiction over public law controversies outside constitutional issues, in particular over challenges to administrative acts.

§2. Legal Family and the Slovak Law

2. The Slovak legal order was based on the Hungarian custom law as late as 1950. In the period between the twelfth and sixteenth centuries, the Hungarian custom law was mostly influenced by Germanic law, Canon law, and Roman law. After the emergence of the Austro-Hungarian Empire, the Hungarian custom law came under the influence of the Austrian law and in the period of the so-called Bach's absolutism (the 1850s), the Austrian law was even fully introduced in the Hungarian part for a short time.

In the fifteenth century, there were increased tendencies and demands to codify the custom law. A notable Hungarian lawyer named Stefan Verböczy was entrusted with that task, and in 1514, he produced the work *Opus tripartitum iuris conseutudinae incclyti Regni Hungariae partiumque adnexarum*. However, the Tripartitum was not enacted so it did become a code.

After 1514, there were numerous attempts to elaborate a collection of laws, and the best known of them is a three-volume collection of laws from 1696 entitled *Corpus Iuris Hungarici*. This collection was incorporated in the system of custom law.

As a consequence of 1848 revolutionary events, the principles of feudal law were brought to an end. With that, the Hungarian custom law based on *Tripartitum* and *Corpus Iuris Hungarici* was virtually abolished. The 1811 Austrian Civil Code was introduced in Hungary.

This state of affairs only lasted until 1860 when the Hungarian custom law was made effective again on the basis of the Emperor's decree from 20 October 1860.

As the Austrian law could not be fully eliminated, it was necessary to determine the scope and the manner of restitution of the Hungarian law. The task was assigned to the so-called Judexkurial Conference in 1861, which worked out and approved in the same year the Temporary Rules of Procedure, but which were not enacted, and their legal binding effect was derived from the authority of the custom law that adopted these rules.

After the break-up of the Austro-Hungarian Empire, Slovakia became part of the Czechoslovak Republic. On the basis of the Act No. 11/1918 Sb. z. a n., the existing legal order was adopted so the Hungarian custom law was effective in Slovakia from 1918 until 1950.

In 1950, the first Czechoslovak Civil Code No. 141/1950 was adopted.

The legal culture and the constitutional foundations as a whole in the territory of what is now the Slovak Republic were then, at the beginning and until 1950, under the influence of the Hungarian custom law.

After 1918, the constitutional system of the new Czechoslovak Republic adopted some elements of the French Constitution of the Third Republic. The general system of private law remained untouched until 1950 when the Czechoslovak law was subject to the influence of the Soviet legal system. Under the Communist regime (1950–1989), the democratic principles of civil law were distorted. After 1989, the Slovak legal system has again found its original roots, but some of its new codifications are more and more inspired by modern European codifications, particularly of German origin.

According to politicians' wishes, the draft of the new Slovak private law, which is being prepared at present, is supposed to be inspired by several models: the German, the Dutch, and the new Hungarian one, among others. The Slovak and Czech legal cultures still remain close to each other, even if some of their concrete expressions have diverged in parts of legislative and judicial solutions since the break-up of Czechoslovakia in 1993 – despite the harmonizing influence of the European law. This development will be completed after the adoption of new civil codes (the draft of the Slovak Civil Code is being finished as this monograph goes to print).

§3. Primacy of Legislation in the Slovak Legal System

3. In the Slovak Republic, law-making must proceed by means of legislation. There is therefore no customary law as such. Customs can be considered only in those cases in which a statute refers to them.

Other important sources of law are international treaties and international covenants of human rights. Those international treaties and covenants have a direct binding effect upon and supremacy over the national statutes.

The Constitution takes precedence over the statutes. The priority of the Constitution is especially important in respect to provisions protecting fundamental individual rights. All ordinary statutes are void or may be declared void insofar as they violate any fundamental constitutional rights. The priority of statutory law over administrative regulations results from the subordinate position of the administrative agencies in respect to the legislature. Furthermore, an administrative agency may promulgate legal rules only on the basis of a formal statutory delegation of power that specifies the content, the purpose, and the scope of the authority so granted. Duties and obligations can be imposed only by statutes, not by administrative provisions.

Two rules govern the conflict between legal rules otherwise having the same priority: a recent law prevails over a prior law; specific rules prevail over more general ones.

§4. The Position of the Judiciary

4. In Slovak law, the Court decisions and writings are not considered to be sources of law; nevertheless, they often have a decisive influence upon courts and administrative authorities. In this context, rules of interpretation are of great importance, such as an interpretation of words, a grammatical-logical interpretation, an interpretation of intention, an analogy of a statute, an analogy of a legal principle, or principles of natural law.

In order to guarantee a uniform case law, only the Supreme Court can give its opinions on the unification of the case law. Such opinions do not have the force of a generally binding source of law. As a rule, however, they are followed by all courts.

A special position is granted to the Constitutional Court. The Constitutional Court may declare void any statute or its provisions insofar as they violate the Constitution or an international treaty having supremacy over the Slovak law. The Constitutional Court may declare void any administrative regulation or its provisions insofar as they violate the Constitution or an international treaty having supremacy over the Slovak law. The decisions of the Constitutional Court are the so-called negative source of law. The Constitutional Court is not a law-making authority, but it can declare void the existing sources of law or their parts.

§5. Distinction Between Public Law and Private Law (Administrative Contracts)

5. Until 1950, civil or private law was understood as all that was not public law; thus, it included even commercial law. Legal writers for some time used the term 'private law' in a narrower sense, excluding commercial law. However, between 1950 and 1989, the distinction between 'private' and 'public' law was considered inappropriate. After 1989, a new discussion on this topic was opened. An important step towards solving the problem of distinction between private and public law was to establish necessary criteria of such distinction. The first of them are criteria of involvement and the second, criteria of power.

According to the criteria of involvement, private law respects freedoms of an individual while public law protects public interests and the public order. Such classification dates back to Roman law, as expressed by Ulpianus: *'Publicum ius est, quod ad statum rei romanae spectat; privatum, quod ad singulorum utilitatem'*. According to the criteria of power, public law expresses the dominant position of the state authority in protecting public interests and the public order. The Slovak legislators accepted the dualism of public and private law again after 1991 in several modifications of the Civil Code. A renewal of dualism of private and public law in the Slovak legal system was regarded as an instrument of reinforcing legal guarantees of natural or artificial legal persons and of preventing the state from unauthorized interventions in private business activities.

6. The present Civil Code reflects the principle of the Civil Law regulation declaring that the parties of Civil Law relationships are equal in their rights and obligations. This equal position is reflected in the following way:

- none of the parties of a civil law relationship is authorized to impose unilaterally any duties or to transfer unilaterally any rights on the other one;
- none of parties of a civil law relationship is authorized to decide disputes concerning rights and duties of another participant as created from the civil law relationship. Such disputes can be decided solely by competent authorities, in particular by courts or in special cases by arbitrators if statutes provide so. The participants of any litigation are equal in their rights (§2, Article 2, Civil Code).

The principle of equality is now undoubtedly one of the basic principles of legal regulation of private law. The public authority can influence private law relationships or create their inequality under restricted and special conditions:

- a particular interest to protect special categories of civil law relationships, for example protection of children or protection of persons who are not capable to defend effectively their own interests;

- protection of some participants of a civil law relationship against economic supremacy of other participants which could lead, respecting formal equality of the participants, to devaluation of the social purpose of the legal relationship, for example consumer protection, abuse of the dominant position, etc.

7. Due to the distinction between private and public law, the contract law is influenced in the same way. Apart from typical private law contracts concluded between parties with a private law status, there are contracts concluded within a public law regulatory framework (administrative contracts):

(a) Between public authorities, for example communities, states or its regions. These administrative contracts are concluded in the situations when statutes do not directly establish a subordinate position between the persons in question. In such cases, rules of private law are applied to administrative contracts.
(b) Administrative contracts can also be applied as a part of public law relationships created between public authorities and private individuals. In such cases, administrative contracts can partially reflect the contractual autonomy of participants. For example, a decision on a subsidy granted by a public authority to a private individual can be accompanied by an administrative contract providing for particular conditions of such a subsidy, etc.

§6. Distinction between Civil Law and Commercial Law (Commercial Contracts)

8. As mentioned above, the Czechoslovak legal system during 1950–1989 did not make any distinction between private law and public law. Thus, no discussion was possible about the broader sense of private law or about its narrower sense excluding commercial law. Starting from 1948, an extensive state control and central planning of the economy were introduced, and in 1964 the Economic Code more or less established an administrative regulation of economic contracts. Those were more similar to the above- mentioned administrative contracts than to commercial contracts in the sense of Continental legal systems.

After 1989, the concept of 'private law' was renewed in Czechoslovakia but in a very broad sense including commercial law as well, as a reaction to its previous absence in our legal system. Amendments to the Civil Code in 1991 and the introduction of a new Commercial Code in 1991 created a dual codification of private law. The Civil Code represents a general codification of private law including contract law, while the Commercial Code is a special codification for commercial contracts and for persons of commercial relationships such as commercial companies and commercial cooperatives.

While the application of the Commercial Code to specific persons, such as commercial companies, is relatively clear, the application of the Commercial Code to specific contracts, such as commercial contracts, is not without difficulties. The category of commercial obligations is defined in §261 of the Commercial Code as follows:

(a) Obligations between entrepreneurs (businesses – B2B), that is between persons involved in continual business for profit.
(b) Obligations created between the state, or its entities, or other legal entities of Public law and an entrepreneur (business) in the framework of business activities of the latter for the purpose of public interest.
(c) Obligations where the character of parties is not decisive but the Commercial Code provides for special types of contracts which should be governed by commercial law, for example, contracts on letter of credit, banking guarantee, traveller's cheques, lease of a share of a company, etc.

When a contract is concluded between other parties than those who should conclude it according to the Commercial Code, or when there is a contract not directly specified by the Commercial Code as a commercial contract, the parties may agree to conclude such a contract according to the Civil Code or according to the Commercial Code. A choice between the Civil Code and the Commercial Code, if possible, must be expressed in a written form. Both types of contracts provide for protection of the consumer in terms of general provisions of the Civil or Commercial Code.

– 9

Introduction to the Law of Contracts

§1. Definition of the Law of Contracts

9. In the Slovak legal system, contract law is a part of the law of obligations. It is a part of broader private law, comprising a set of legal rules on contracts (obligations). The central term of contract law is obligation, by which the following is usually understood:

- obligation as legal relationship (obligation in a broader sense);
- obligation arising from this legal relationship (obligation in a narrower sense).
- Other fundamental terms of contract law are:
- claim and debt;
- creditor and debtor.

Under the contract law, a claim is a subjective right of one party (creditor) to the contract relationship to demand from the other party of the same relationship (debtor) a certain performance, that is, demand from him to give something, to act, or to refrain from acting, that is, omitting. If the claim becomes payable (mature) it principally becomes a title, that is, unless a voluntary performance was provided by the debtor it may be successfully claimed in a court or in an arbitral tribunal. The debt (obligation in a narrower sense) is a corresponding obligation (a duty) of a party to the contract (the debtor) to provide the other party to the same obligation relationship, that is, the creditor, with the performance demanded by him and promised by the debtor in consistency with the claim. The creditor is generally the party to the contract who has a claim (rights), and the debtor is the party who has a duty (obligation) to satisfy such a claim.

Binding legal relationships arising from contracts may be classified according to the branches of private law into civil contract law and commercial contract law, and possibly also into contract law of other branches (e.g., labour contract law). From another point of view, contract law distinguishes general contract law and specific contract law. Further, binding legal relationships were historically classified according to its source of formation: obligation relationship arising from contracts and obligations enforceable from torts.

The most frequent and typical ground for formation of an obligation relationship is a contract. It is habitual to distinguish provisions on obligations arising from contracts and provisions on some quasi-contracts, for example: benevolent intervention in another individual's affairs (acting for another individual's benefit without agency, *negotiorum gestio*), public promise, and public tender. Contract is a fundamental notion of contract law. It is a bilateral or a multi-lateral agreement that gives rise to a binding legal relationship or that has some other legal effect.

§2. Historical Background of the Law of Contract

10. When the independent Czechoslovak state came into existence in 1918, the new Czechoslovak Republic continued to apply these generally valid codes in the Czech lands. In Slovakia, Hungarian law was applied in the sphere of civil law. From the very beginning of the independent Czechoslovak state, work on the new Czechoslovak Civil Code was started. The draft was ready in 1938, but due to the Nazi occupation and to the post-war development in Czechoslovakia, it never entered into force.

After the liberation of Czechoslovakia in 1945, and particularly after the Communist takeover in 1948, the former legal system gradually underwent radical changes as a result of the transformation that occurred in the whole social and economic system. A new Civil Code was adopted in 1950 (No. 141, 1950 Col.), which replaced the ancient Hungarian custom law.

The new Civil Code, adopted in 1964 (No. 40, 1964 Col.), was strongly influenced by the then-existing political trends. It was based on the theory that 'civil law regulates only economic relationships arising among socialist organizations and citizens and among citizens in the process of satisfying their own needs'. The rest of private law was divided into several branches, each of them with a special codification – family law (Family Act No. 94, 1963 Col.), labour law (Labour Code No. 65, 1965 Col.), economic (commercial) law (Economic Code No. 109, 1964 Col.), and private international law (Private International Law Act No. 97, 1963 Col.). In the period of 1964–1989, it was impossible to apply the Czechoslovak Civil Code to international trade due to its strong political orientation. Therefore, in Czechoslovakia there existed at that time in fact two Civil Codes – the 'internal' Civil Code (No. 40, 1964 Col.) and the 'Civil Code for international trade' – International Trade Code (No. 101, 1963 Col.). The Economic Code No. 109, 1964 Col. was applied to 'internal' economic contracts, that is, to 'contacts among the socialist organizations'.

11. After 1989, when Czechoslovakia was re-establishing its democratic order and the rule of law, it became necessary to rebuild its legal system as a whole. As early as 1989 and 1990, the Constitution was substantially amended, in particular as regards democratization of the society and basic freedoms in personal and property relationships. The first stage of the reconstruction of private law meant substantial amendments to the Civil Code. The International Trade Code was abolished; the Family Act and the Labour Code were amended. The Economic Code was abolished as well, and commercial law was restored in the country by a new Commercial Code (No. 513, 1991 Col.).

In the 1990s, and in particular after the split of Czechoslovakia in 1993, the development of private law was focused on two matters: to prepare the accession of the Slovak Republic to the EU with regard to the necessary approximation of its legislation, and to make a general reform of the Slovak private law in compliance with modern needs. The first task was accomplished by the date of accession of the country to the EU on 1 May 2004. The second one – the general reform of the Slovak private law – already went through its principal stage and a draft of the new Civil Code has actually been accomplished. The new Civil Code should become a dominant and general source of private law with links to special legislation in different areas of private law, particularly the Labour law (a new Labour Code was adopted – No. 311, 2001 Col.), Family law (a new Family Code was adopted – No. 258, 2005 Col.), and the Commercial Code (a draft of new Commercial Code has been prepared). Codification of international private law should remain unchanged, except for the influence of the European international private law. This part of the reform is to be achieved by 2012.

The Slovak contract law should be essentially changed through the re-codification of the Slovak private law. The development of the re-codification of whole Slovak private law, which started before more than twenty-two years, depends to a considerable extent on political circumstances and on the personal situation of re-codification board. The draft of wording of the new Civil Code was elaborated in the past a few times, but it has not been accepted by the drafting board and by the Ministry of Justice so far.

The Slovak lawyers are in agreement that the new Civil Code should include also the commercial juridical relations (arising between businesses, B2B). The Slovak lawyers achieved also the consensus about structure of Civil Code, which should be divided into five basic parts. The most extensive discussion holds namely about obligation law, including contract law. Coincidentally, the contract law should just constitute the most extensive part of new Civil Code.

There were the above-mentioned difficulties, that brought the drafting board to the solution to elaborate first of all the re-codification of civil procedural law. This unusual operating procedure was nevertheless put into practice: from 1 January, three essential legal acts of civil proceedings came into force:

- Act No. 160/2015 Col., Civil Proceedings Act.
- Act. No. 161/2015 Col., Uncontroversial Civil Proceedings Act.
- Act No. 162/2015 Col., Administrative Proceedings Act.

The minister of justice established, after national elections in the year 2016, the new drafting board for the work upon the new Civil Code. The board is very large and works under governance of its presidium. The members of board are divided into working groups, headed by president of the group.

In month May 2016, the working groups were tasked with working out the text of particular parts of Civil Code, and submit it within due delay. The deadline was not kept and subsequently the functioning of the board was – let's hope that temporarily – interrupted.

§3. Classification of Contracts

12. Classification of contracts is based on the same criteria as classification of any other juridical acts:

(1) according to the number of parties – bilateral or multi-lateral contracts;
(2) according to the value of the transaction – reciprocal or gratuitous;
(3) according to the form – formal or informal;
(4) according to the subject matter we recognize:

- contracts with monetary performance where at least one party's performance is provided in money;
- contracts with non-monetary performance.

Particular contract types may be classified as follows:

(1) Preliminary contract obliging one or both parties to conclude, within a certain period, a contract with a content agreed beforehand (§50a, Civil Code, §289–292, Commercial Code).[1]
(2) Contracts creating an obligation relationship – typical ones, that is, 'named' contracts (as described in the Civil or Commercial Code), or atypical ones, that is, 'unnamed' contracts (not explicitly described in the Codes), or mixed contracts (§491, Civil Code). Concluding unnamed, or mixed contracts by parties is based on their freedom to contract; however, they must not be inconsistent with law, good morals, and intentions of the respective rules of law.
(3) Contracts to guarantee obligation relationship.
(4) Contracts causing change in an obligation relationship (e.g., contract on assignment).
(5) Contracts causing termination of an obligation relationship (e.g., agreement on setting off).

§4. Contracts and Torts

13. Obligations as relationships may also be created by unlawful acts – torts. Tort in Slovak law is a private/civil non-contractual liability arising out of damage resulting from a breach of a legal duty that exists by virtue of the society's expectations

1. From the case law:

Ruling 4 Obo 225/2000: If only one of the parties to the contract is obliged from a preliminary contract concluded pursuant to §289, Commercial Code, then only that party has a duty to conclude the contract (published in Collection of Rulings, No R 111/2001).

Ruling 1 Cdo 107/2006:

Prelimary contract (§50a, Commercial Code) is only between the parties to such a contract. If the future seller fails to fulfil an obligation resulting from a preliminary contract and subsequently he concludes a sale contract for the transfer of real estate with a third party this does not invalidate the sale contract in question pursuant to §39, Civil Code. Rights and duties resulting from the preliminary contract will be discharged due to frustration.

regarding interpersonal conduct rather than by contract or other private relationship. The essential elements of tort are: existence of a legal duty, breach of that duty, and a causal relationship between the conduct and the damage. Torts are breaches of liability (no matter whether this is a liability created by contract or another liability *ex lege*). Torts are violations of rights and statutes. The Slovak Civil Code describes torts under the general provision: 'Everyone is liable for damage caused by him while breaching a legal obligation.'

Torts may be divided according to fault:

- caused by fault;
- without fault.

Torts may also be divided according to consequences:

- torts causing threat of breach of legal relationship;
- torts causing breach of legal relationship.

The Slovak law classifies the general rules of the law of contract and the law of unlawful acts – torts – under the heading of the law of obligations.

In the Slovak Civil Code, important consequences of both unlawful acts and failure to perform an obligation are regulated in a uniform way.

In some cases, the Slovak law limits liability in a different way than non-contractual liability (a different regulation on legal capacity or a different period of limitation).

§5. Contract and Quasi-contract

14. The recent Slovak Civil Code did not accept the Roman classification of the sources of obligation in '*contractus, quasi-contractus, delictus, quasi-delictus*'. The Slovak Civil Code states that all obligations arise from juridical acts, in particular from contracts as well as from damage caused by a person, unjustified enrichment, or other facts laid by law. In the Slovak law, a great majority of obligations in practice are created by contracts (*ex contractu*). There are, however, some unilateral juridical acts that could create an obligation. Such obligations, similar to obligations created by contracts, are called quasi-contracts. This term is not described by the Slovak Civil Code.

The Slovak Civil Code contains provisions on contracts, unlawful acts, and some other sources of obligations, namely, agency without mandate (*negotiorum gestio*) and unjustified enrichment.

In the view of similar consequences, quasi-contracts are, for example, public tender (§847 and fol., Civil Code), commercial public tender (§281 and subsequent provisions, Commercial Code), public promise (§850 and subsequent provisions, Civil Code), promise of indemnity (§725 and subsequent provisions, Commercial Code).

§6. Contracts and the Law of Property

15. We can find in the Slovak law a distinction between absolute rights and relative rights. An absolute right is a right to property that can be upheld against everyone. A relative right is connected with a person (all rights to the performance of an obligation are relative rights).

Absolute rights are rights to property (ownership), copyright, patent, etc. There is a closed system of real rights whereas the system of obligations is open.

A majority of private law contracts are obligation contracts, that is, contracts leading to the formation, a change, or the termination of a contractual obligation relationship. There are, however, contracts leading to the formation, a change, or the extinction of real rights.[2]

These are exceptional under the Slovak law, as a result of the two-phase construction adopted for obtaining ownership (or the formation of another real right), namely, in relation to real property. The first stage means the formation of a contract; the second stage is registration of such a contract by a State authority – Land Register.

§7. Contract and Trust

16. The trust as a specific legal conception is not known in the Slovak law.

There are some cases of legal relationships on the basis of which a person – owner of a certain property – is under a contractual duty to manage and administer this property on behalf of someone else. An example can be the Slovak Organization of Copyright administering copyright on behalf of authors.

Various specific institutions such as *fideicomissum*, *Treuhand*, etc., are not known in the Slovak law.

Entrusting the care of property to another person is possible in the Slovak law only (usually) through an innominate contract for obligation or through establishing an artificial legal person (e.g., a foundation) for that purpose.

§8. Good Faith and Fair Dealing

17. As stated above, the Slovak Civil Law is governed by three equity principles of contract law:

> Under §39, Civil Code, contracts must not be contrary to good morals (contra bonos mores). The term 'good morals' is commonly interpreted as a set of moral rules applied together with the formal legal norms. The contracts that are contrary

2. Towards the relationship between a contractual right and the right to title; *see* the ruling 1 Cdo 31/2000: 'If the seller has breached a contractual duty resulting from the sale contract and because of that the right to title was not recorded in the Cadastre and he will transfer the same real estate to another person this breach does not invalidate the latter sale contract (in the sense of §39, Civil Code) which resulted in allowing registration of the title in the Cadastre.'

to good morals are void, that is, they are deemed to be concluded but without any legal consequences.

The term 'good faith' (bona fides) is applied under Slovak law either as a general principle or a prerequisite of fairness in the conduct of parties to contracts or as a psychological category, expressing the psychological state in which the party to contract is not aware of legal errors related to the contract. In the latter sense, good faith applies only when expressly referred to by law.

In commercial contracts, the principle of 'fair dealing' is applied. It is similar to the principle of good morals in civil law but is of a slightly different nature and the principal difference concerns legal consequences. If a court concludes that a contract or its performance is contrary to fair dealing it is bound to refuse granting court protection to such acting.[3]

§9. Style of Drafting

18. The law of contract is based on some general principles of which the central one is equality of parties. Another primary principle is that of freedom to contract as an expression of autonomy of will. It is expressed, for example, in Article 2, al. 3 of the Slovak Charter of Fundamental Rights and Freedoms, which stipulates that 'everyone is authorized to do anything what is not prohibited by law'.

Freedom to contract means predominantly the freedom to conclude or not to conclude a contract; to select a contractual party; to select the type of contract; to determine the content of the contract or the content of obligation relationship to be formed by a contract; to denote the form of the contract; and finally, to refrain from a contract under stated conditions:

(a) Freedom to contract – Party autonomy may be restricted by law only through imposing a duty to conclude a contract, for example, a contract on energy supply, on public transport, on radio and television broadcasting. Certain restrictions of freedom to contract may also arise from voluntary contracting (e.g., *pactum de contrahendo*).
(b) Free choice of the contractual party may be excluded due to public interests (e.g., regulation on sale of the goods).
(c) Contractual parties may agree on other types of contracts, different from those stipulated by law; there is no numerus clausus, a limited number of contracts allowed (cf. options for atypical contracts – §51).
(d) Freedom to contract – Party autonomy is established by mandatory rules of law that may not be excluded or diverted from by the parties in contracting. Mandatory rules are not very frequent; at present, they serve to protect the weaker party of the contract (e.g., consumer protection – see e.g., the provision of general consumer contracts or the particular provisions on liability for faulty goods sold in shops).

3. Cf., for example, a ruling of the Supreme Court of the Slovak Republic according to which the agreed amount of interest rate, if it is not in contradiction with the principle of fair dealing, may be higher than interest rates usually required by banks when they grant credits (R 6/1998).

(e) Contractual parties can conclude contracts in any form – explicitly (in oral or in written form) or in another way which does not give rise to doubts on what the party wished to express; unless certain formalities have not been stipulated by statute or agreed by the parties.

§10. Sources of the Law of Contract

19. Law of contract is a part of private law. Legal regulation of contract law may be found in several statutes:

(a) Basic contract law regulations of the general nature are laid down in the Civil Code, Act No. 40, 1964 Col. At present, obligation relationships are provided in its two parts:

   - Part 6 'Liability for damage and for unjustified enrichment', that is, torts and quasi-torts.
   - Part 8 Contract law in which Head I contains the general part of contract law, Heads II – XXI contain provisions on particular obligations (relationships) arising from juridical acts, mainly contracts, that is, contract law and law of quasi-contracts.
   - The above-mentioned provisions of the Civil Code are rather inconsistent as a result of gradual amendments to the Civil Code, mainly concerning provisions on liability for damage, preceding provisions on contract law, and the general part of obligations is placed in the part providing only for contracts.

(b) An extensive set of obligation rules is contained in the Commercial Code, Act No. 513, 1991 Col. Obligations are dealt with in Part 3 on business obligation relationships.

(c) Further legal rules contain provisions on some specific kinds of obligations not regulated in the codes mentioned above. These are for example:

   - Act No. 618, 2003 Col. on copyright, the related rights and some other acts of law as amended (Copyright Act).
   - Act No. 527, 1990 Col. on inventions, industrial designs and innovations.
   - Act No. 444, 2002 Col. on industrial designs protection.
   - Act No. 116, 1990 Col. on lease and sub-lease of non-accommodation (non-residential) facilities.
   - Act No. 566, 2001 Col. on securities.

Part I. General Principles of the Law of Contract

Chapter 1. Formation

§1. Agreement and Quid Pro Quo (Reciprocity)

I. Offer and Acceptance

20. Under the Slovak law, contracts are bilateral or multi-lateral juridical acts arising from bilateral or multi-lateral manifestation of will. Such expressions of will should be of an identical content and should express mutual assent.

One of the juridical acts is a proposal to conclude a contract – an offer. Offer is an expression of will, by which the offeror proposes the offeree to conclude a contract on the subject matter given in the offer. The offer contains two elements: the first one concerns the contractual assent, the second one the determination of the content of the future contract. The offer is effective from the moment it has been delivered to the offeree. The offer, even though it is irrevocable, may be revoked by the offeror, if the revocation reaches the offeree before the offeree has dispatched an acceptance.

The offer may not be revoked:

- within the time limit stated for its acceptance, unless the right to revoke prior to the expiry of that time is implied in the offer;
- if irrevocability is stipulated in the offer.

The offer is binding for the offeror, although not for an indefinite time. First, the time limit stated by the offeror for the acceptance of the offer must be considered. An offer may not be revoked for the reasons stated above. But an offer irrevocable expires:

- by the expiry of the time stated for the acceptance;
- by the expiry of a reasonable time taking into account the nature of the contract proposed and communication means used by the offeror for dispatching the offer;
- by delivering the offeree's rejection of the offer to the offeror.

Unless accepted immediately, an oral offer is terminated if not stated otherwise in the offer. The time limit set for the acceptance by the offeror in a telegram begins to run from the moment the telegram has been submitted to the post office. If the date is stated in the letter, the time for the acceptance runs since that date, or if such a date is missing, since the date stated on the envelope. The time limit for the acceptance, stated by the offeror by phone, telex, or other means enabling immediate communication begins to run from the moment when the offer reaches the person intended.

The second juridical act is the acceptance. Accepting an offer, the offeree manifests his will to the offeror to accept his offer and concludes a contract with him on the subject matter as stated in the offer. The acceptance may be carried out by a declaration or a conduct by the offeree (e.g., by performance). In any case, it must be a manifestation of will carried out on time. The acceptance becomes effective at the moment when the consent with the expressed offer reaches the offeror. A conveyance contract does not require any prompt declaration of acceptance by the offeree; a written declaration in the same document containing the offer is sufficient. The acceptance of an offer made to the absent offeror is effective only after the reply of the offeree has reached the offeror.

The acceptance may be revoked if the respective revocation has reached the offeror sooner than or simultaneously with the acceptance. A late acceptance is nonetheless as effective as the acceptance if, without undue delay, the offeror informs the offeree that it is treated as an effective acceptance. However, an answer expressing the acceptance but containing supplements, reservations, restrictions, or other changes (modified acceptance) is a rejection of the offer and it is deemed to be a new offer (counter-offer).

The moment of conclusion of a contract is described by §44, paragraph 1, Civil Code, under which a contract has been concluded at the moment when the acceptance of the offer has become effective. Silence or inaction in itself does not imply the acceptance.

II. Intention to Create Legal Relations

21. Offer and acceptance are juridical acts, that is, manifestations of will to conclude a contract. Thus, an offer and acceptance must contain:

(a) manifestation of will;
(b) declaration of the extent of the manifestation of will to conclude a contract;
(c) recognition of the manifestation of will by the rules of law;
(d) consequences following the intention expressed by the manifestation of will.

(a) Manifestation of will is an essential concept, implying unity of two components: will and manifestation.

The will is an element of a juridical act together with awareness of legal consequences of the acting person as the subjective aspect of the manifestation of will.

The will designates a mental category and expresses an inner mental relation of the acting person to the intended legal consequences. As a result, the will must understand the significance of a juridical act created in a qualified manner. The requirement that the will should be manifested in a certain way recognized by law denies or reduces legal relevance of the will of such persons who, due to the lack of mental capacity or maturity, are unable to properly predict the consequences of their will manifestation. Therefore, the manifestation of will made by a person incapable of rational decision-making due to his lack of mental capacity or his age has no legal effect.

The will may be manifested in any manner enabling to recognize its content. According to manifestation of will we can distinguish:

- an explicit manifestation;
- an implicit manifestation.

An explicit manifestation can be performed orally, in writing, or by sign language. With regard to increasing use of modern methods of recording, processing and transfer of information, using of agreed or usual codes, signs, etc., is possible as well. For some juridical acts, a certain manner of explicit manifestation is prescribed (e.g., a written form of a contract). Implicit manifestation of will is a manifestation communicated in other than an express manner, for example, by acting (tearing the testament, etc.) or by omission (expressing the will not to make the contract by inaction of the offeree in reaction to the offer). Omissions are legally relevant only if there is inaction or silence in situations where acting is necessary.

In certain cases of inaction, civil law establishes a presumption or a fiction of a real will; however, such will is not apparent or demonstrable (§47, paragraph 2, Civil Code):

– The requirement to declare the extent of manifestation of will means that the will must be intended to result in the rise, a change or the termination of legal relation (rights and obligations).

Various views within the civil law theory have been expressed involving the extent of will to cause legal consequences. The prevailing and most logical concept is that manifestation need not comprise all legal consequences of an act. It is not possible for a lay person (non-professional) to comprise by his will all detailed legal consequences that may be attached to his will by legal rules. Therefore, a will of a person including essential consequences is sufficient. Further consequences will necessarily arise under law if determined by cogent rules (conditioned by non-mandatory provisions unless excluded by the parties as agreed). Therefore, a person need not be clearly and entirely aware of all legal consequences; it is sufficient if he intends certain (fundamentals) legal consequences to arise.

From the above stated, it follows *a contrario* that where there is no will to create legal consequences there is no juridical act. Acts of social service are not juridical acts for the same reason. For example, to refrain from smoking in places where smoking is not prohibited by law is not of legal nature; therefore such a manifestation of will is not intended to create legal consequences:

- Manifestation of will gives rise to legal consequences only if such a manifestation of will is recognized by law (approved). Therefore, recognition of will by legal rules is another concept of juridical acts. If this concept is missing, the manifestation of will is not deemed relevant under law. The concept is related to the word 'law' comprising the term 'juridical act' as defined under §34.
- For a juridical act, it is not sufficient that manifestation of will is recognized by rules of law, but certain legal consequences must be attached to it by law. Moreover, it is stated under (b) that these consequences are those intended to arise by the acting person (if concerning fundamental consequences). In other acts, for example, in illegal acts as well as in persons' behaviour which is not determined by will but which is subject to law, consequences also arise, however, not by the will of the acting person but by force of law.

III. Consideration (Gratuitous Promises; Natural Obligations)

A. Consideration

22. The Slovak law does not know the doctrine of consideration as it is known in the *common law system*.

B. Gratuitous Promises

23. Gratuitous promises to perform something exist in the Slovak legal system as exceptions, the standard form of such promises being a deed of donation and a public promise.

Unilateral contracts attach the debtor's position to one party only and the creditor's position to another party. Apart from all subsidiary rights and obligations of the debtor and the creditor, for example, a duty to provide cooperation in performance and right to cooperation to be provided, the subject matter of the contract will be one performance only. An example, and in fact an exception to value relations governed by civil law of contracts, is the obligation established by a gift covenant (deed of donation).

Another type of a gratuitous contract under Slovak law is a public promise (*see* Part II, Chapter 19).

A special position in contract law is held by a mental reservation. It is belief of a party to the contract that in relation to concluding a contract another advantage will be granted; this belief, however, is not expressed towards the other party in a significant manner. This mental reservation is not legally binding under Slovak law and is not a part of contracts.

C. 'Natural Obligations'

24. The Slovak civil law distinguishes a subjective right, that is, the ability of a person to behave in a legal way, and a claim, that is, the property law based on its enforceability by the state power, exceptionally exercised by an authorized person.

The claim thus comprises the following:

(a) presents enforceability of a subjective right against the will of the obliged person;
(b) its existence is linked to a subjective right;
(c) presents an option to use state power or self-help for the claim enforcement.

In most instances, the Slovak law of contract provides subjective rights through claim, an exception being a group of the so-called *natural obligations*. These are rights that cannot be enforced by the Court or by an authorized person. These include rights that are subject to period of limitation, rights from wagering and games that are not permitted or organized by the state, and rights arising from loans for such wagering and games (§455, paragraphs 1, 2, Civil Code).

Civil law recognizes as exceptions such obligations that the legislator refuses to provide with enforceability through state or personal enforcement, that is, obligations that do not constitute a claim. It is in fact the type of incomplete rules (*leges imperfectae*) that are denoted as natural obligations (*obligationes naturales*) under contract law. These obligations are characterized by the two following features:

- lack of the ability to demand performance by enforcement. Performance may be exercised only through a voluntary act of the debtor;
- if performance was exercised in this manner, its return cannot be demanded under the stipulation on unjust enrichment.

Natural obligations are:

- obligations arising from loans in wagering and games;
- obligations for which time period limitation (prescription) has expired;
- obligations invalid due to lack of formalities.

IV. Modifications of the Contract

25. The Slovak civil law recognizes the following changes in content and subject matter:

(a) agreement of modification (*cumulative novation*);
(b) debtor's delay (mora debitoris);
(c) creditor's delay (mora creditoris).

(a) Agreement of the Parties (*Cumulative Novation*)

26. With regard to the principle '*pacta sunt servanda*', the parties may, by agreement, modify their mutual rights and obligations. In fact, the parties conclude a new contract in order to modify the former one.

Cumulative novation, as a form of an obligation relationship change, may be considered an instance where the parties agree on a new obligation that will substitute the current obligation.

As the current obligation continues to exist, so does also the surety of the obligation. If the surety's consent has not been obtained for the novation, the surety is entitled towards the creditor to demur all he could have demurred prior to the novation agreement becoming effective.

(b) Delay of Debtor (*Mora Debitoris*)
The Term and Its Appearance

27. The Slovak Civil Code stipulates that a debt (obligation) must be fulfilled on time and properly for the obligation to be discharged by performance. If the debtor has not fulfilled his debt on time and properly, he is in delay. Both performance terms must be given cumulatively to deem the obligation discharged by performance. So a debt fulfilled on time but having legally relevant flaws has the same effects as a debt not performed without the time stated.

Besides the general stipulation for debtor's delay in performance arising from an obligation, the Civil Code specifies special legal consequences for the particular types of obligations. We will deal with them in relation to the respective obligation types.

Legal Consequences of a Debtor's Delay

28. Debtor's delay causes a change in the obligation content, resulting either in a change of creditor's rights and debtor's duties or in the rise of new creditor's rights and new debtor's duties. These may be further classified as follows:

- Once the debtor is in delay, the creditor is entitled to determine additional reasonable time for performance. If the debtor does not perform within this time either, the creditor is entitled to withdraw from the contract.[4] If the performance is severable, the creditor may withdraw from the contract effective only in a part of the performance. Legal consequences of the withdrawal involve all types of contracts, that is, also the contracts registered by a state notary's office in the respective procedure. Thus the debtor's delay does not affect his obligation to fulfil the debt before the creditor's withdrawal from the contract has become effective.
- The right to withdraw from the contract as mentioned in the previous paragraph does not involve the so-called fixed contract. In the case of an obligation where the time of performance was stated quite strictly and it is obvious beyond any doubt from the contract or from the nature of things that the creditor loses his economic interest upon delayed performance, under the Civil Code such a contract is cancelled *ex lege*. Only in the case where the creditor insists on the performance, he must announce it without an unnecessary delay to the debtor and thus the obligation continues to exist.
- In the case of a monetary claim, the creditor is entitled to demand interests for delay when the Civil Code or implementing provisions do not stipulate a duty to

4. After the expiry of an additionally provided period, the seller may withdraw from the contract because of the buyer's failing to pay the sale price even if this has not been agreed by the parties (the ruling Cpj 29/1997).

pay fees for delay for the particular case (the amount of interest and fees for delay are stated by the respective implementing provision).[5] The Commercial Code contains newly the specific regulation of the interests for delay (*see* § 369a–369, Commercial Code).

- If the debtor is in delay with the performance, the risk of loss, damage or destruction of a thing has passed upon him, unless the damage would have occurred anyway.
- The debtor's delay entitles the creditor to claim compensation for the damage caused by the delay. In the case of monetary performance delay, the debtor will be liable only up to the amount, which is not covered by the interest for delay or by fees for delay.

(c) Creditor's Delay
The Term and Its Appearance

29. Creditor's delay occurs when the creditor has not accepted any performance from the debtor, or when the creditor failed to provide the necessary cooperation to the debtor in performing the obligation.

Legal Consequences of Creditor's Delay

30. Creditor's delay results in the following:

(a) during the time of the creditor's delay the debtor's delay may not occur;
(b) if the thing was a performance, the risk of loss, damage or destruction of the thing lies on the creditor for the time the creditor is in delay;
(c) if costs or a damage incur to the debtor during the time of the creditor's delay, the creditor is bound to compensate;
(d) if the nature of the debtor's performance so allows, the debtor can fulfil the debt through an official deposit.

---

5. The amount of interest from delay in paying a financial debt is determined by the Government Decree No. 87, 1995 Col.; every year it is a twofold amount of the basic interest rate (previously discount rate) established by the National Bank of Slovakia and payable on the first day of delay in paying a financial debt. This amount does not change during the period of the debtor's delay (ruling 4 Cdo 193/2005).

The question whether the interests on late payment are added to the debt and further interests are calculated on the basis of that increased debt is dealt with in the ruling of the Supreme Court according to which the late payment of interests does not give rise to any right to further interests on late payment (R 70/1995).

It follows from the provision of §517, para. 2, Civil Code, in connection with §3, Government Decree No. 87, 1995 Col., that only the upper limit of interests on late payment that cannot be exceeded is mandatorily established (ruling 1 Cdo 58/1998).

The provision of §3, Government Decree No. 87, 1995 Col. concerning the amount of interests on late payment cannot be applied to relationships regulated by the Commercial Code (R 20/2003).

§2. Formal and Evidence Requirements

I. Formal Requirements

31. Under the Slovak law, contracts can be made, unless stipulated otherwise by law or agreed by the parties, in a form that does not give rise to doubts about the content of the will as manifested by the parties to the contract.

The forms of a juridical act may have various forms, the basic classification being into written or oral ones. The Civil Code does not specify the oral form. The written form is further classified into a simple form and that of an official record. The simple written form requires a written expression and a signature. Typically, the writing of contracts means that the text of a contract is embodied in a document. The text itself may be made by any technical means (unless expressly stipulated for some juridical acts that it must be made in one's own hand, the signature must be in one's own hand). Replacing signature by technical means is admissible only where it is ordinary (§40, paragraph 2). If the juridical act has been carried out by electronic means, it may be signed electronically under §40, paragraph 4 of the Act No. 215, 2002 Col. Requirements of the written form are met if a juridical act has been carried out by telegraph, telex, or by electronic means enabling recording of the juridical act and denoting the person who has carried it out. In contracts, manifestations of the parties may be made in different documents, but in real property conveyance, the expressions of the parties must be included in the same document. In the cases stated by law the written form is made more restrictive by the signature attestation as prescribed (e.g., signatures of the parties to the contract for the transfer of share in business pursuant to §115, paragraph 3 of the Act No. 513, 1991 Col. as amended). The form of the official record is a qualified written form, at present it is a public notary's record.

The cases where the parties are bound to submit to one another a written confirmation about a juridical act or to make a record must be strictly distinguished from a written form (e.g., §141, paragraph 2). However, validity of juridical act is not linked with such requirements.

Lack of the form required by law results in the contract being void, lack of the form as agreed on is related to the contract being voidable (§40a, Civil Code).

The accepted performance based on a juridical act being void due to the lack of formalities (arising either from law or from an agreement) is not deemed unjustified enrichment. This cannot be deemed a validation of a juridical act because by the provision quoted only one of the possible consequences of a void juridical act is excluded, that is, a duty to return the unjustified enrichment obtained through a void juridical act.

Tender

32. Tender is a specific manner of concluding a commercial contract enabling to select the most suitable offer from the bids. Therefore, tender is used mainly for contracts where one of the parties is a public authority and where the tender is obligatory, declared and conducted exactly according to the rules stipulated by a special law. In commercial obligation relationships, it is the case where a person (the announcer) on his own will announces the tender for the most suitable proposal to conclude a contract. The tender is not yet an offer for making contract; it is only a call to submit offers for its making. The call for tenders done in the form of a tender is related to legal consequences. In announcing tender, the terms of competition are required to be published.

II. Contract Under Seal

33. The 'obligation' contract under seal is not mandatory in the Slovak contract law. *See* more in V. Function of Notary and Notarial Instruments.

III. 'Solemn' Contracts

34. Solemn contract as a manner of concluding contracts is unknown to Slovak law. An exception is marriage solemnization, which, however, is not generally deemed a contract.

IV. Evidence Requirement

35. As for a special form of contracts required by law or agreed on by the parties, *see* the previous text.

Only in cases stated by law do some declarations of the parties to the contract require a special form of the so-called official record, which can either be a public notary record or, in some cases, also a record made by bailiffs under the Judgment Enforcement and Execution Act. (*See* more in section V. Function of the Notary and Notarial Instruments.)

V. Function of the Notary and Notarial Instruments

36. Under the Slovak law, the notary is a public clerk, his duties involving, among others, drawing up contracts in the cases where an official form of the notarial record is required by law or by agreement of the parties.

This form is required by law in the following instances:

- generally for all juridical acts of such persons who are unable to read or write, not even while using a technical device enabling them to get acquainted with the text of the document to be signed and to sign them in turn by their own hands;
- where it is specified by law (cf. forms of testament, establishing certain types of companies).

The position of the notary is regulated in the Notary Act. The notary is appointed for life by the Notary Chamber. The notary candidate must have a university degree in law and a preliminary practice. There are quantitative limits for establishment (imposed by the Notary Act and by the decisions of the Notary Chamber. The notary is obliged to comply with high professional standards and must exercise due care in the execution of his activities. The notaries are subject to disciplinary jurisdiction executed by the Notary Chamber.

The Notary Act furthermore includes provisions in the form of notarial records and other requirements that must be met. The notarial record has the value of an authentic act (public instrument).

The notary has the power to issue a special notarial act (e.g., a contract) with an execution clause, which may serve as a writ to execution.

The task of the notary lies especially in the field of law of matrimonial property (marriage contracts, etc.), law of artificial legal persons (establishing, modification, transfer, and termination of companies, associations, foundations, etc.), law of succession (e.g., testamentary dispositions), and law of immovable things.

VI. Burden of Proof

37. The distinction made between ‘obligation of means’ and ‘obligation of results’ as a general concept is unknown to Slovak law.

Slovak law distinguishes situations where the expression of will and manifestation of will are not identical, that is, the cases when the content of will is different from what follows from its manifestation. As will manifestation as a feature of a juridical act necessarily presumes compliance of will with its manifestation, in the case of inconsistency of will and its manifestation an essential feature of the juridical act is missing. Various inconsistency variants of a will and its manifestation may occur, one of the basic criteria of their classification being the relationship of inconsistency and the awareness of the acting person. Thus deliberate and accidental inconsistency of will and its manifestation may be distinguished.

a. Deliberate inconsistency of will and its manifestation is one-sided where one party’s will and its manifestation are inconsistent and both parties are aware of it.

One-sided deliberate inconsistency of will and its manifestation arises as a mental reservation or a one-sided simulation.

Mental reservation (inner reservation) means that the acting person includes a reservation in the will he manifests but does not explicitly manifest that reservation. Thus the will and its manifestation of the acting person are not consistent to some extent; the acting person is aware of it, but the other parties of the juridical act or third persons are not, because the reservation is of inner nature, not being explicitly manifested.

One-sided simulation (pretending) of *some* will is of similar nature; the acting person manifests a different will from the one he really has. He realizes this fact but he pretends to other party and third parties to have the will he has manifested.

The consequence of one-sided deliberate simulation results from the fact that the will manifested is not serious. Therefore, it results in the juridical act being void (§37). This voidness can be claimed only against the party who was aware of the will and its manifestation inconsistency. However, the party, having presumed that the act was made seriously, may claim it as if it were valid (cf. §41a, paragraph 2).

A shared deliberate inconsistency of will and manifestation occurs when in bilateral or multi-lateral juridical acts all parties manifest something different from what they really want. Their real wills are consistent, so are their manifestations, but there is no consistency between their real wills and real manifestations. It is a simulation where the parties pretend to carry out a juridical act (relative simulation). A simulated (fictitious) juridical act suffers from inconsistency of will and its manifestation; moreover, the will manifested is not serious. Therefore, they are sanctioned by being held void under the Civil Code. Also in this case voidness of the act may not be claimed against the party who considered it unveiled. A veiled juridical act is a dissimulated juridical act. If this veiled juridical act corresponds with the will of the parties and meets all the requirements, it is valid (§41a, paragraph 2).

– Accidental (unknown) inconsistency of will and its manifestation is a mistaken manifestation.

As for mistakes, errors, *see* Part 1, Chapter 2.

§3. Liability and Negotiations

I. Pre-contractual Liability

38. For the parties to be able to conclude a contract properly several fundamental terms must be met, including:

(a) terms concerning the entity involved, that is, legal personality and capacity of a person to make the contract in question, or the capacity of the person representing the party in concluding the contract;
(b) the title of the party to the contract subject matter, that is, title to the thing to be sold under the contract.

Other pre-contractual liabilities basically are not generally required under the Slovak law.

There are in the Slovak Civil Code pre-contractual duties between a business and a consumer in the consumer contracts:

- information duties (general duty to disclose information about goods and services, specific duties for the business delivering goods or services to consumers, duty to provide information when concluding contract with a consumer who is at a particular disadvantage, information duties in distance communication, information duties when concluding consumer contract by electronic means. Generally, the information must be clear and precise and expressed in a plain and intelligible language;

- duties to prevent input errors;
- duty to negotiate in accordance with good faith and fair dealing (good morals-good manners).

II. Breakdown of Negotiations

39. Generally, the persons are free to negotiate and are not liable for failure to reach an agreement.

Termination

40. Contractual negotiations may be terminated prior to conclusion of the contract, the basic principle being that the offeror or offeree are both bound by contractual manifestations. It is necessary to distinguish the possible terminating of the offer by the offeror and offeree (about this subject matter, *see* more above in Chapter 1, §1, I. Offer and Acceptance).

In Slovak Civil Code, *clausula rebus sic stantibus* or as a term in *pactum de contrahendo* are not stated. But in the Commercial Code, we can find the *clausula rebus sic stantibus* as an instrument of the deliberation of one of the contractual parties from the duty to conclude a future contract.

The Slovak law does not state the concept of *culpa in contrahendo* as the written norm, either. But at the beginning of the twenty-first century, under the influence of the ECJ case law, the Slovak Constitutional Court accepted the principle of legitimate expectation, subsequently applied by courts, that in the cases when a person refuses to make a contract without a sufficient reason and the other person suffers loss then such a person is awarded damages.

Chapter 2. Conditions of Substantive Validity

41. Contracts arise upon two unilateral addressed juridical acts. For their rise and for their validity, it is necessary that their addressing be mutual, identical in content, and expressing assent to contract. (For more about the right to revoke or reject the offer or acceptance, *see* above in Chapter 1, §1, I. Offer and Acceptance).

The contract content will be specified mainly by the offer, and for some types of contract the law prescribes which essential parts must be contained in the contract in question, otherwise it does not exist (cf. contract for sale and purchase as an agreement on the subject matter and the price). The contract may also contain the content of the contract on a future contract, the non-mandatory rules included in law, etc. The instant of concluding the contract is stipulated by §44, paragraph 1, under which a contract is made upon the instant when acceptance of the offer becomes effective. Silence or inaction themselves do not imply acceptance.

The same principle also applies to carrying out multi-lateral juridical acts where expression of will of more than two parties is required, and the substance of which is also assent and mutual and harmonious will of all parties to the contract.

Sometimes another fact is required (e.g., assent of other parties or ruling of a relevant authority) to be added to the unilateral will manifestation, or manifestations of will of two or more parties.

Formation and subsequent existence of a juridical act is one of the prerequisites for its validity.

Formation and validity must be distinguished from a juridical act when becoming effective, that is, from a situation when effects of a juridical act are connected with such a will manifestation by a rule of law. In the majority of cases, the rise, validity, and effect of a juridical act fall within one instant. Only in specific cases, the law binds the effect of a valid juridical act to meeting further requirements. Such process is regulated in the present Civil Code under §47, paragraphs 1 and 2; for the cases where ruling of a respective authority is necessary for a contract, the contract takes effect only upon that ruling. Unless an application for the respective ruling has been filed within a three-year term following the conclusion of the contract, the parties are deemed to have withdrawn from the contract (§47, paragraph 2). Withdrawal from the contract is effective *ex tunc*, that is, at the time of the conclusion of the contract. Within an established period of time, it is necessary for the application to be submitted to the respective authority. The purpose of this provision is to prevent further existence of contracts that did not become effective and are thus purposeless (in 1983–1992 this construction was broadly applied in registering contracts by state notaries).

Essential Elements

42. For the contract as juridical acts to have capacity to give rise to proper legal consequences it is necessary – in addition to existence of its respective terms – to meet quality requirements, the fundamental elements, or essentials of a juridical act. These essentials usually involve the following:

(a) capacity of the parties;
(b) will to contract;
(c) manifestation of will;
(d) will in relation to expression;
(e) subject matter.

(a) Capacity of the Parties

43. The prerequisites of the parties to carry out juridical acts are, first, their capacity to exercise rights and take liabilities, and, second, their capacity to act. General capacity of a natural person in juridical acts (capacity to act) is regulated by §§8–10, of juridical person by §§18–20a, Civil Code. The effects of incapacity are contained in §38, Civil Code.

If a party lacks capacity to act, the juridical act becomes void. The law does not expressly stipulate this effect; however, it is implied in the nature of this essential condition. Such a case may occur with some juridical persons whose capacity is of a specific nature (extent).

The lack of capacity to perform juridical acts results in voidness of the respective juridical act. It will be so in the case of minors if they carried out a juridical act inconsistent with their limited capacity, in the case of persons incapacitated by a court ruling or persons with limited capacity. A juridical act carried out by a person not incapacitated or restricted in capacity by a court ruling will also be void if such a juridical act was performed in a state of mental disorder that made the person incapable to act (§38, paragraph 2). This provision relates to cases of temporal mental disorder (including drunkenness) as well as the cases in which the Court could have ruled on incapacitation or a restricted capacity but it has not done so yet.

(b) As for the Will Essentials, Usually the Following are Named: Existence, Freedom, Seriousness, Lack of Error

Existence of Will

44. The requirement of real will means inevitability of its existence. In this regard, including real will as an essential condition among the essentials of the juridical act is redundant as it overlaps with the necessity of will existence as a feature of a juridical act. If there is no will, no juridical act is formed. Therefore, such a juridical act must be deemed non-existing (*non negotium*). However, the Civil Code does not know this notion and therefore it may only sanction lack of will by voidness.

The cases where the will is missing are clear but sometimes the will of an acting person appears to be present, even though it is not. An example is the will enforced by physical duress comprising physical pressure upon the party who expresses the will of the person exercising duress upon him instead of his own. This means that the will of the acting party does not exist here.

Freedom of Will

45. Free will is freedom to act, that is, freedom of a party to decide in what legal relations he/she will participate through juridical acts the basis of which is their will. Free will does not exclude general limitations and conditions stated by law for juridical acts.

Under civil law theory, free will is deemed excluded when the following circumstances are present: physical duress, wrongful threat, and distress.

By physical violence, another person forces the acting person to express the will of the person exercising violence upon him, instead of his own. It is of no significance if the violence comes from the other party or from the third party. Neither is decisive whether the other parties to a juridical act were aware of physical force exercised upon the party or not. For physical duress to be legally relevant, it must be illegal and a causal relationship must be found between it and the expression made by the person under pressure, that is, the performed expression must be the result of duress. As physical duress excludes the will of the acting person, the fundamental element of a juridical act is missing and therefore such an act is futile and as such void under the Civil Code.

Wrongful threat is an illegal threat affecting the will of a party, causing in him a reasonable fear of a threat of injury. In this manner, the will of the person under threat is created contrary to his real will. The difference between physical violence and wrongful threat is that in wrongful threat the person under threat expresses his will, but such a will is deformed by a wrongful threat. While in the case of violence the acting person has the only option, that is, to express the will of the person exercising violence upon him, he has two options in the case of a wrongful threat, either not to submit and to express his own real will, or to submit and express the deformed will. Avoidance of the contract entered due to the wrongful threat is possible also in the case where such wrongful threat was exercised by a third party, even if the other party of the contract was not aware of the third party's duress.

Wrongful threat is relevant under law while satisfying the following conditions:

- The threat must be wrongful, that is, the threat comprises something that is not allowed (e.g., to cause bodily harm) or the threat comprises something that the threatening person is entitled to use, but not for the purposes to make another person to perform a certain juridical act (e.g., by filing a complaint against somebody for an actually committed offence if the contract is not made).
- There must be a causal link between the threat and the expressed manifestation; the threat must incite fear influencing directly the will of the person under threat.
- The threat must be of such intensity as to be able to give somebody real fright. The seriousness of the threat to cause fear is judged individually considering both the subjective situations of the acting parties and the particular circumstances involved.

Wrongful Threat Makes a Legal Act Voidable

46. Free will is excluded also by distress, which means an objective condition of the acting person regardless of how or due to whom the distress has arisen. Distress is an economic, social, health, or another condition that alters by its existence the true will of the acting person in such a way that it forces the acting person to carry out a juridical act under strikingly disadvantageous terms. As the condition of distress is of objective nature, the party benefiting from it need not be aware of it. However, if a party caused the other party's distress, he will be liable for its unfavourable consequences.

Strikingly disadvantageous terms are judged individually. In contract to mutual performance, the decisive aspect may be an economic equivalence of the performances provided. This aspect is not the only one; strikingly disadvantageous terms may have various forms and may also occur in gratuitous contracts.

The party who entered contract under distress can withdraw from it.

The will of a party is not serious if the acting person does not want to give rise to legal consequences that are related with such a will and its manifestation under law. A broader interpretation of seriousness of will – when the will does not intend to invoke legal consequences – also includes mental reservation, simulation (see the explanation on accordance of will and manifestation).

Lack of serious will has to be assessed as an error leading to a futile legal act. Pursuant to the Civil Code the lack of seriousness of will results in voidness (§37).

From the view of legal certainty of third parties, it is necessary to consider whether non-serious will is binding. If lack of seriousness is clear to the other party, too, naturally the other party understands that the will is not directed to a juridical act and does not intend to result in legal consequences. If it is not obvious, protection of the other party relying on seriousness of the will must be secured. Three concepts of meeting this requirement can be found in civil law. One part of the legal theory considers such an act void, but its consequences are to be effective in relation to the relying party based on the expressed manifestation. It means that here the manifestation is preferred despite the will quality. The theory of trust protection considers the juridical act as non-existing, but in relation to the rightfully trusting party, the same legal consequences will come as from a valid act. Most common is the concept of consequences of liability related to §37, Civil Code, so the consequences of a juridical act will not arise but instead liability consequences will arise under §42, Civil Code, presuming the acting party was liable (cf. §420, Civil Code).

An error – similarly to lack of serious will – presents discord between legal consequences that the party intended to give rise to and the consequences actually arising. The error of will means wrong or insufficient awareness of legal consequences arising from a juridical act (this differs from an error of expression which is a discord of will and expression). The consequences of legal invalidity relate only to a certain qualified error of will (such error is deemed legally significant). Other errors cause no such legal consequences. An error is of legal significance if:

- it is concealed (the party acting in error is not aware of it);
- the other party shared in its rise;
- he incited it intentionally;
- he incited it in another way or he must have known about it: in this case an error must be based on a fact that is decisive for the juridical act to be carried out, the so-called substantial error (mistake to content).

Substantial error may concern the following circumstances:

- legal grounds (*error in negotio*) – the party incorrectly presumes that the will is directed to a certain act while it is another act in fact (the exchange of deed of donation instead of contract for sale);
- the subject of a juridical act, either its identity (*error in corpore*) the party thinks to be buying the thing A, but subject of the purchase contract is subject B, or the properties of the subject (*error in qualitate*) – the party is buying, for example, an antique which is not an antique, though;
- persons (*error in persona*) involving a change of the person;
- other circumstances without which a juridical act would not be carried out.

Error of will may result in voidability (until 1991 the option of withdrawal was stipulated).

(c) Essential Requirements for Manifestation are Intelligibility, Definiteness, and in Some Specified Cases Also a Form

47. The expressing of will is unintelligible if its content is not clearly said and it is not possible, according to an interpretation, to find out what have been in fact expressed.

Unintelligible manifestation of will cannot give rise to legal consequences, and therefore it is sanctioned by voidness (§37).

Civil law is based on the principle of no-form expression, which means that a juridical act may be carried out in any form, unless specifically stipulated by law. Even if no formalities have been prescribed, the parties may agree to carry out a juridical act in a certain form. Therefore, formalities can be imposed by statute or by contract.

The forms of juridical acts may be various, the basic classification being into written and oral ones. The oral form is not prescribed by the Civil Code. The written form is then classified as simple and by official record. The simple written form requires the act to be recorded in writing and a signature appended. Typically, the written form means that the content is given in a document. The text itself may be made by any technical means (unless stipulated that they must be made in one's own hand). The signature should be in one's own hand. If replaced by technical means, it is admissible only where it is ordinary (§40, paragraph 3). If a juridical act is performed by electronic means, it may be signed electronically under Act No. 215, 2002 Col. The written form is made permanent if a juridical act is carried out by telegraph, telex, or electronic means, enabling recording the content of the juridical act and denoting the person who carried it out. In contracts, expressions of parties may be in different documents; only in the case of contract on conveyance of immovable property the expressions of parties must be placed in one document. The written form in the cases as specified may be made stricter by a prescribed certified signature (e.g., signatures of parties to the contract for the transfer of share in business pursuant to §115, paragraph 3 of the Act No. 513/1991 as amended). The form of the official record is a qualified written form; at present, it is a public notary's record. The following forms are required by law:

- in general for all juridical acts of those who cannot write or read, not even while using special equipment enabling them to get acquainted with the content of the documents signed, and to sign it by their own hands;
- in specially stipulated cases (cf. the form of the last will, the establishing of a limited liability company by a single person must even be in the form of a notarial record).

Lack of the formalities prescribed by law results in voidness while lack of the agreed formalities results in voidability.

Voidness due to lack of form is related to special situations, not occurring in other reasons for voidness. Under §455, Civil Code, accepted performance, based on a juridical act that is void as a result of lack of form (both under law and under contract), is not deemed unjustified enrichment. It cannot be said that it is a validation of a void legal act because by the stipulation quoted above only one of the possible consequences of a void legal act is excluded, namely, the duty to return unjustified enrichment obtained from a void legal act.

(d) The Essentials of the Relation of Will and Its Manifestation, and Their Conformity

48. Civil law analyses in detail the situations where the will and its manifestation are in discord, that is, the cases when the content of will is something different from what follows its manifestation. The will manifestation as a feature of a juridical act necessarily presumes a concord of the will with its manifestation; in the case of discord of the will and its manifestation a fundamental feature of a juridical act is missing. Various combinations of will and manifestation discord may occur; one of the essential criteria of their classification is the relation of discord and the awareness of the party. Accordingly, known and unknown discords of will and manifestation are recognized.

A known discord of will and manifestation is one-sided, when the will is in discord with the manifestation of one party, or common (bilateral or multi-lateral) when the will and the manifestation are in discord on all sides and both parties know about it.

One-sided known discord of will and manifestation comes as mental reservation or one-sided simulation.

Mental reservation means that the party makes a reservation in the will he manifests without explicitly expressing that reservation. It means that the will and manifestation of the acting person are in discord to a certain extent; the acting person is aware of it but the other parties to the juridical act or third parties are not because the reservation is of an inner character, it is not explicitly manifested.

One-sided simulation (pretending) of will is of a similar character; the party manifests something different from his true will; he is aware of the situation but pretends before other parties to have the will he is manifesting.

The consequence of one-sided intentional simulation follows from the fact that the will expressed is not serious. Therefore the result is voidness of the juridical act (§37, Civil Code). This voidness may, however, be claimed only against the party who was aware of the discord of the will and manifestation. On the contrary, the party who presumed the act to be serious may claim it as if it were valid (cf. §41a, paragraph 1).

A common (shared) known discord of will and manifestation is given when in a bilateral or a multi-lateral juridical act all parties express something different than they want in fact. Their real wills are in accord, so are their manifestations, but there is no concord between their real will and the manifestations expressed. It is a simulation when the parties pretend to carry out a juridical act even though they want to carry out none (absolute simulation) or they pretend to carry out a certain juridical act to disguise another juridical act (relative simulation – *dissimulation*). Simulated juridical act suffers from discord of will and manifestation; moreover, the will manifested is not serious. Civil Code therefore sanctions it by voidness. Also in this case voidness of the act may not be claimed against the party who deemed it unconcealed. Concealed juridical act is a dissimulated juridical act. If this concealed act in law is consistent with the will of the parties and satisfies all conditions, it is valid.

Unknown discord of will and manifestation is an error of manifestation. Also here one-sided and two-sided discords may be recognized.

Unilateral unknown discord arises when the acting person's will is in discord with its manifestation in a unilateral juridical act or the will and its manifestation of one party in multi-lateral juridical act. These are the situations where the actor expresses that he wants something but in fact wants something else without realizing error in his manifestation (slip of a tongue – *lapsus linguae*, mistake in writing, etc.).

Similarly to cases of errors of will, various types of errors in manifestation are recognized:

- error in a juridical act – the acting person has expressed a will for a juridical act to be carried out, even though he in fact intended to carry out another act (e.g., instead of the intended donation he expressed the will to make a contract of purchase);
- error in the content of a juridical act – the error in the effects to be brought about by the juridical act – for example, error in time, place and manner of performance;
- error in subject may have various forms, for example, error in identity of the thing, error in kind (quality), property and amount of a thing;
- error in the person of the contracting party, for example, erroneous person gifted under a deed of donation.

If manifestations of will of two or more parties are in discord, the consent to contract is missing and thus a juridical act in theory may not arise. This is true if the discord concerns a substantial matter but discord does not prevent a juridical act to arise if it is only formal and may be resolved by an interpretation. The non-substantial elements of a juridical act affected by discord will be governed by the relevant stipulations.

Two-sided discord gives rise to voidability, too.

(e) Subject Matter Must Be Possible and Allowed

49. The possibility of subject matter in a juridical act should be understood as the possible conduct of the party in correspondence to rights and obligations arising from the juridical act. Most often, it will be performance. Possibility of performance arising from a juridical act is objectively an inevitable requirement of validity of a juridical act. If the subject matter of a juridical act is performance that cannot be provided, such an act cannot be legally binding (voidness).

The possibility of subject matter of a juridical act must not be made identical with the existence of a thing. It is not the thing that is impossible but the performance related to such a thing, for example, donation of such a thing is impossible, etc. When the subject matter of performance is a generic thing, the performance is actually impossible in practice, too. However, there can be an exception, namely, with the things that ceased to be produced or imported and are no more available in the period from the moment of making the offer and the actual contract making (e.g., in mail-order sale and purchase).

Impossibility of the subject matter of a juridical act results in its voidness, but the impossibility must be absolute (physical). This also concerns the cases when performance is so extraordinarily difficult that with the regard to good morals the owing party cannot be rightfully expected or demanded to overcome the obstacles. Any other level of impossibility of performance cannot be deemed an impossible performance. Also, such performance is not impossible that is only relatively impossible, that is, such that is impossible only due to subjective reasons, that is, only in the view of the owing party.

Impossibility must be initial, that is, it must exist upon the rise of the juridical act. If such impossibility arises only after the juridical act occurred, it results in termination of the existing obligation.

An allowed juridical act means that such act is legally possible, that is, it is judged according to the rules of law. A not allowed subject matter results in the juridical act being void. Examples are the subject matter being inconsistent with law, evading law or being contrary to good morals:

- Inconsistency with law is evident mainly when certain behaviour is expressly prohibited by law. Inconsistency with law may concern the content, too, which is not expressly worded but it is implied in the stipulation. Inconsistency with the purpose of law cannot be judged so easily and in the sphere of civil law §3 paragraph 1 Civil Code must be applied.
- The subject matter of a juridical act evades law if it does not violate directly the requirement given by law but is inconsistent with the objectives of the given law. For example, according to an older court decision, a contract under which a criminal offender transferred his property in order to frustrate enforcement of forfeiture was declared void. Law is evaded by such a contract in spite of the fact that the contract itself is not contrary to any provision of law.
- Inconsistency with good morals means that the subject matter of a juridical act is not contrary to law or evades it, but the social objectives of the act or relationship to arise from it are breached.

In the sphere of civil law, the principle 'everything is allowed what is not banned' is applied.

Chapter 3. The Content of a Contract

§1. General Explanation

50. The content of a contract means legal consequences of forming, changing, or terminating a legal relationship, or rights and obligations. The content of a legal relationship is thus stated (even though indirectly) as forming, changing, or terminating upon a juridical act.

The content of a contract is determined by the parties within their autonomy of will, but it must respect certain cogent stipulations of legal rules, either stipulating content essentials or excluding elements in some juridical acts. The contract content may also be influenced by the decision of a respective authority as well as by the content of non-mandatory rules unless their effects were not excluded by the acting person's conduct.

Contract terms are classified according to their frequency and their legal relevance into substantial, regular and incidental:

(a) Substantial terms are such that are unconditionally required. These terms are given by legal norms (e.g., subject matter and price in contract for sale) and can be specified by the parties, that is, they are of subjective nature (enabling the parties to denote such elements essential which they themselves consider important).
(b) Regular terms are such that occur as a rule, but their absence has no effect on the rise and validity (e.g., agreement on the time and place of performance).
(c) Incidental (subsidiary) terms are such that arise only incidentally and irregularly. These are mainly conditions, time determinations, and some others.

Conditions are such subsidiary provisions by which the consequences of the juridical acts are made dependent on unknown circumstances (conditional juridical acts). Such an uncertain circumstance may be a future fact that is not known to the parties whether it will occur or not, or a fact that will certainly occur but the parties do not know when, or a past fact about which the parties do not know that it had already occurred.

For more about the conditional contracts, *see* below in §3.

Time fixing as a provision in a juridical act is similar to a subsidiary condition. It means that effects are conditioned on the expiry of time. Unlike a condition, in the case of time fixing it is certain that the time stated will expire and the effects of the juridical act will come into existence or terminate. Time fixing may be of two types: in the first case, the effects of a juridical act will come into existence only after a certain time; in the other case, the effect of a juridical act will terminate after the expiry of the fixed time (about time-limited rights and obligations *see* more below).

Consequences

51. Consequences of a contract may be the rise, a change, or the termination of a juridical act (rights and obligations). These consequences concern persons affected by the juridical act and things that denote legal relations (rights and obligations) established, changed, or terminated by the contract.

As a rule, the contract has effects only for the parties who made it. This conclusion arises also from the character of civil law regulation method, where the party in a civil law relationship may not one-sidedly interfere with legal relations of other individuals, except for the cases given by law. The exception is a contract in favour of a third party (*pactum in favorem tertii*). It is a contract where one party (the debtor) promises the other (the creditor) to perform in favour of a third party. Such a case is an insurance contract for insuring property, life, or health of third parties.

As for the subject matter, the contract has consequences only for the legal relationship directly involved. An exception is accessory relations linked in their existence with prime legal relationships (as a rule, *security* relations on securing a claim).

Grounds and Consequences of Invalidity

52. Such consequences are linked to the contract inconsistent with rules of law and can be divided as follows:

a. Futility (Nullity)

A juridical act is deemed futile (*non negotium*) that misses one of the substantial features. Basically, it is an act that only seems to be a juridical act but misses, for example, will, expression, etc. The Civil Code does not define futility; the cases that in theory are reasons for the juridical act futility are sanctioned by voidness.

Invalidity

Invalidity in relation to a juridical act or a legal relationship means that the juridical act or the relationship is void or has been avoided. There are two types of invalidity, voidability and voidness.

The voidability as included under the Civil Code is rather a distinct form of the general notion of invalidity.

Voidness

53. Void juridical acts are deemed existing but invalid if certain requirements or essentials sanctioned under law by voidness are missing. No legal consequences arise from such juridical acts for the parties or third parties. It is characteristic that voidness arises directly under law *(ex lege)* without the necessity to claim the consequences by either party. Voidness may be claimed by anyone legally involved, not just by the parties. The court will not consider voidness ex offo. Grounds for voidness include inconsistency with law, good morals, evading law, lack of freedom and serious will, uncertainty and unintelligibility of manifestation, etc.[6]

The effects of voidness of a juridical act can be considered according to time and subject matter.

As for the time, voidness is effective as a rule *ex tunc*; the juridical act is void since its origin. The voidness is effective immediately. Voidness persists even though the grounds of such voidness became extinct later; a void juridical act may not become valid later. Voidness cannot be rectified through confirmation of an obligation. Only the so-called conversion is possible, which means that if a void juridical act complies with the essentials of another juridical act it may have consequences of that juridical act.

As for the extent, the effects of voidness are considered according to whether the whole act, or only its part, is void. The solution is found in §41, Civil Code, under which only that part of an act that is affected by the grounds for voidness is void. The part of the act not affected remains valid being a separate whole.

Voidability

54. The essence of voidability is the fact that a juridical act that is deemed valid induces legal consequences as if valid by the time its invalidity has been claimed or declared by the respective authority. Voidability is taken into consideration only upon the objection brought by the entitled party. Pursuant to the Civil Code, it is the person affected by such an act, that is, the party to a juridical act or a third party, who was affected by the ground of voidability. A person who has caused invalidity may not object to the voidability of juridical act.

The question of the qualified claiming of the effects of voidability is not quite satisfactorily resolved in the legal theory. There is an opinion that the principle of equality of the parties must be respected and therefore it is possible to induce consequences of voidability in two ways:

(1) The part affected by voidability will claim voidability in relation to the other party by a unilateral juridical act who will accept the objection and they both together take measures for removing negative consequences of the voidable juridical act.
(2) If the other party will not accept the objection, the party wishing consequences of voidability to occur must file a complaint with the court for invalidity to be declared. In such cases, legal consequences of voidability will occur only on the grounds of the court decision.

6. From court rulings:
Contract of donation made with the purpose of settling a debt owed by the donor in relation to the donee is a void legal act (ruling 4 Cdo 33/2005).
If a contract of insurance which includes terms of insurance refers to non-existing parts of general insurance terms, then such a contract is uncertain and non-understandable and therefore void pursuant to §37, Civil Code (R 48/2000).

However, a different opinion has been accepted by majority of legal writers (which also prevails in court practice and is supported by the authors of this text) based on distinguishing direct and indirect voidability. In direct voidability, claiming voidability by the party entitled is sufficient. For the effects of voidability to arise an out-of-court notice is sufficient by which the entitled party claims voidability (it is a real one-sided addressed juridical act). The voidability becomes effective upon the instant when the notification reaches the other party or all the parties to the act. In the case of indirect voidability, the voidability of a juridical act must be declared by the Court. The Civil Code establishes direct relative voidability.

The possibility to claim voidability is bound to a certain time limit. The Court practice, however, holds that this right of the party is subject to the expiry of a three-year period. This time limit begins to run on the day of carrying out the juridical act.

The grounds of voidability of juridical act are in comparison with grounds of voidness less serious, and therefore personal incentive of the party affected is expected to avoid the consequences of the invalid act. This also includes lack of the agreed formalities for the expression of the juridical act, lack of consent of another party, etc. (§40, Civil Code).

Voidability affects juridical acts in respect of time and subject matter, too.

As for the time, voidability as a rule is effective since the beginning *(ex tunc)* but unlike voidness only on the condition that the respective claim for voidablity has been made. Unlike voidness, in the case of voidability, a validation may be admissible. If the flaw that might have lead to voidability was removed or rectified, invalidity cannot be claimed (e.g., by a subsequent consent with the subject matter of the juridical act that exceeds a usual management of common property of spouses).

Withdrawal from an Invalid Act

55. Withdrawal is a unilaterally addressed juridical act of the entitled party intended to prevent the effect of the act. An invalid act is deemed existing and valid and thus causing legal consequences; however, one can withdraw from it. The option to withdraw from an invalid act is available exclusively to the entitled party, that is, the party affected by the invalidity with which the option to withdraw is linked.

The effects of withdrawal become effective at the moment when the expression of withdrawal has reached the other party, while effective *ex tunc*, that is, retroactively since the time when the juridical act was carried out, unless prescribed by law or agreed by the parties otherwise. The effects of invalidity of a juridical act by which the entitled party withdraws from an invalid act occur automatically (per se), and are not dependent upon the decision of the other party or the Court. The Court may only check whether the juridical act by which the entitled party withdraws meets the given terms or not. The effects of withdrawal are definitive, validation or a following confirmation of the act is not possible. The effects of withdrawal might be removed only by carrying out a new juridical act.

As for the extent, withdrawal has the effect identical to invalidity, even though this is not expressly stipulated by law. The opinion prevails that withdrawal is reasonable only to the extent to which the juridical act is affected by a respective flaw, provided that the part to remain valid is a separate unit.

The grounds of withdrawal due to invalidity of the juridical act are regulated by the Civil Code. It is, for example, the case when a contract was concluded in distress with strikingly disadvantageous terms. Withdrawal is admissible also in other cases not resulting from invalidity of a juridical act.

Contesting

56. Contesting of juridical acts means an option to claim legal consequences ineffective only towards a certain person (creditor).

(*See* more below in Chapter 4, §4. *Actio Pauliana.*)

Liability for Invalidity of Juridical Acts

57. Liability consequences connected with invalidity of a juridical act originate as a consequence of invalidity or withdrawal from an invalid juridical act. The following liabilities are possible:

- mutual restitution duty, that is, the duty of parties to return everything they have received due to the invalid juridical act; general provisions on unjustified enrichment will be applied but it should be noted that performance under the juridical act that is invalid due to lack of formalities agreed by the parties is not deemed unjustified enrichment;
- duty to compensate damage arising as a result of an invalid juridical act.

Influence of the Time on the Legal Relationships

58. Legal relations as well as rights and liabilities may be formed for a period of indefinite duration and as such are unlimited in time, or their duration is limited for a fixed time. There are rights the existence of which is not limited in time (property right, personal rights, personality rights) and for which no time of limitation applies. However, there are rights that are by their nature and designation limited for a certain time. These include the right to use a borrowed thing, right to temporary dwelling, etc. Third group is made by the rights that may be restricted for a certain time but this restriction does not arise from their substance and designation (e.g., restriction of lien for a certain period).

The extinction occurs by the lapse itself on the last day of the time stated, and no further legal facts are necessary.

Preclusion

59. The consequence of preclusion is the extinction of a right that is not exercised in the preclusive period of time. Therefore, two conditions have to be met in order for the right to extinguish:

- lapse of a certain period (precisely given by law);

– failure to exercise the right within this period.

If both conditions have been fulfilled, the following legal consequences of preclusion occur:

– a subjective right extinguishes (along with the claim);
– the respective authority takes into consideration the preclusion ex offo;
– if performance is carried out after the preclusion period lapsed, it is deemed an unjustified enrichment as its legal grounds have become extinct as the result of preclusion (see explanation of unjustified enrichment).

Preclusion terms are rather exceptional in civil law and must be explicitly stated by law, namely, in such a manner that upon failure to exercise the right in this period, the right becomes extinct. These are mostly time limits for claiming liability for damage – deadlines for complaints. Preclusion terms cannot be prolonged and their running is not suspended or interrupted. There are exceptions to this general rule when a certain time is not included in the preclusion period.

Prescription (Statutory Limitation of Right)

60. Unlike the above given consequences of preclusion, under prescription a right does not terminate by lapse of time but is weakened considerably as the claim (actionability) as a part of subjective right becomes conditioned.

A right extinguishes unless exercised within the period stated by the Civil Code. By the lapse of time, the first phase of a right extinguishing is fulfilled if two facts have taken place: the lapse of time and the failure to exercise the right.

When the period of prescription expires the legal relationship between the owing party and the entitled party continues; a subjective right or a claim do not become extinct, only the claim becomes conditioned, that is, dependent on whether the owing party claims the lapse or not. Upon the lapse of time, the right to claim that lapse has arisen to the owing party, if the entitled party demands the performance of his subjective right. The entitled party may claim protection of his right with a respective authority even after the lapse of the statutory time, as his right has not become extinct (unlike in preclusion). The owing party may also voluntarily carry out his obligation even after the lapse of period of limitation and it will not be deemed as an unjustified enrichment of the entitled party as legal grounds for performance have not become extinct.

The second phase of prescription comes at the moment when the entitled party has claimed his right in court.[7] Then it is necessary to distinguish the instances where the owing party has not exercised his right to claim the lapse of time and where he has claimed it. If the owing party has not claimed prescription, the respective authority does not take it into consideration ex offo. Claiming the prescription in relation to the facts from the first phase of lapse causes that the right terminates; the right becomes

7. Pleading the limitations statute is taken into consideration by the Court only when the debtor expressly claims limitation of action; it is not sufficient for the debtor only to express his opinion on the time aspect of the claimed right (R 9/2001).

unenforceable and the respective authority cannot impose it. The subjective right continues to exist, though; it is only considerably weakened (as a result of the claim extinction) existing in the form of a natural obligation. If the performance occurred in this second phase, again it would not be unjustified enrichment.

Not all rights are subject to prescription. With respect to their nature and function, the prescription is not applied to personality rights, personal rights, and personal property rights. Under the law, limitation does not apply to:

- ownership rights;
- lien if there is a debt surety;
- rights from deposits in banks and current accounts if the deposit relationship continues.

Deadlines and Time Limits

61. For the consequences of right extinction, a time prescription is required. The Civil Code stipulates the time prescription in such a manner that it lays down the rules for determining its beginning, length, and specification of some obstacles influencing its running.

The beginning of period of prescription is determined either objectively or subjectively. In general, the beginning is the day when the right could have been exercised for the first time (*actio nata*). Such a day is the one when the right could have been claimed in court for the first time. In theory is it not quite clear when *actio nata* will occur in the case when the performance consists in the duty to suffer something (e.g., to suffer trespassing one's land from the part of others). In the Court practice, it has been held that *actio nata* will only occur when the owing party breaches his duty for the first time, that is, he behaves to prevent behaviour of the entitled party. The other opinion that *actio nata* is the day when the owing party ceased to exercise his subjective right is supported by the interpretation related to easements that will lapse unless exercised within the statutory time limit. The objective beginning of the period of prescription is based on the wording that 'the right could be exercised'. Therefore it is not decisive if the entitled party really was not able to exercise his right or if there was an obstacle preventing him from doing so (a long-term illness, staying abroad), or if he did not know about the existence of that right.

The objective beginning of the period of the prescription is specified in some cases:

- for the rights that must first be exercised by a natural or a juridical person the period of prescription begins to run on the day when the right was exercised;
- for the rights related to performance in instalments, the period of prescription of the individual instalments starts to run since the day of their maturity. If agreed, the whole debt becomes payable if the party fails to pay some of the instalments. The period of prescription starts to run on the day on which the unpaid instalment became due;

- for indemnity, rights the period of prescription begins to run one year after the insurance event;
- for the rights of an entitled heir to demand the inheritance to be released, the period of prescription begins to run since the court decision about terminating the probate proceeding becomes effective;
- in the cases mentioned above the start of running is dependent on subjective facts, which is an expression of protection of the entitled party. This manner of fixing the beginning is used by the Civil Code for the right to compensation for damage and the right to have unjustified enrichment released.

The basic length of the period of prescription under the Civil Code is stipulated three years, under the Commercial Code four years.[8] The length of the period of prescription may vary as stipulated by law.

Shorter periods are stipulated:

- for rights to recovery of damage in the case of a subjectively stated beginning (two years);
- for rights to waive the performance from unjustified enrichment in the case of a subjectively stated beginning (two years);
- for rights arising from transporting (one year) except the right to recovery of damage of transportation of passengers.

A longer period of prescription is stipulated:

- for rights to recovery of damages caused intentionally or damages arising from corruption, that is, breach of obligation resulting from offering or promising bribe by another person than the injured, or as a result of direct or indirect bribe demanding from the injured person (ten years);
- for rights to waive the performance related to easement (ten years);
- for rights imposed by a court decision or another authority (ten years), the same term applies for instalments into which the performance was divided;
- for rights acknowledged in writing by the debtor concerning the ground and the amount (ten years), the same applies to instalments.

When dealing with time it is suitable to deal with the so-called combined times that are those in which several times of prescription (with an objectively or subjectively stated beginning) are applied concurrently in law. In these combinations, various situations may occur; a right extinguishes upon the lapse of a subjectively stated prescription but no later than on the lapse of an objectively stated limitation. The following instances may objectively occur:

(1) The beginning of the subjective term occurs during an objective term and by its lapse the whole subjective term lapses.

---

8. The right to having returned the consideration given according to a void contract is statute-barred after a four-year period pursuant to §397, Commercial Code, the period starting to run from the day when the consideration was given (R 34/2002).

(2) A right extinguishes upon the lapse of the subjective term.
(3) The beginning of the subjective term occurs during the objective term but by its lapse only a part of subjective term has lapsed and another part has lapsed only after its end. The right will extinguish upon the end of the objective term as it is evident from the wording 'a right extinguishes no later than'.
(4) The beginning of the subjective terms occurs only after the objective term has lapsed. The right extinguishes upon the lapse of the objective term, and the subjective term is entirely irrelevant.

The running of the period of prescription is continual since the beginning to the end unless an obstacle occurs with which the law connects the consequences stated. A change in the person of the creditor or the debtor has no influence on the run of the period of limitation. The new debtor may also claim the prescription against the new creditor.

Based on the existence of relevant obstacles, the following effects may occur:

- period of prescription has not begun;
- period of prescription has not ended;
- period of prescription has been interrupted;
- period of prescription has been suspended.

The period of prescription has not started if a fact occurred from which the period of prescription starts to run as usually but due to an obstacle predicted by law the beginning is postponed. Pursuant to the Civil Code, the following situations are included:

- in the case of rights of persons who must have a statutory representation and do not have it, or in the case of rights against these persons;
- in the case of rights between statutory representatives and minors and other represented persons; this does not apply if interests and repeated performance are in question. The same applies to rights between spouses.

If the beginning of the period of prescription has begun and the time runs but during its course an event occurs that causes putting off the end of the period of prescription that would otherwise occur, we can consider the period of prescription not coming to an end. The following cases are included:

(1) If these are rights of persons who must have a statutory representation and have lost it, or rights against these persons. The period of prescription continues to run but it will not end before one year lapses after which a statutory representative will be appointed to these persons, or when the obstacle becomes extinct in another way.
(2) If during the period of limitation such an obstacle occurred, the course of the period of prescription has been interrupted. The parts of the period of prescription that expired before and after the obstacle will be added up. The Civil Code establishes the following cases for period of prescription interruption:

- if the creditor during the period of prescription brings a suit to court or another respective authority to satisfy the claim and duly continues in the proceeding;
- if the right was duly granted and enforcement of judgment was proposed to court or another respective authority;
- if subsequently a situation occurred when exercising a right between statutory representatives on the one hand and minors and other represented persons on the other hand is in question unless there are interests and repeated performance involved.

The cases mentioned here are sometimes designated as interruption in a narrower sense and the cases stated above when the period of prescription does not begin or end are designated as interruption in running in a broader sense.

If such an event occurs that causes suspension of the period of prescription in running, it means that the part of the lapsed period of prescription is not taken into account (becoming legally irrelevant) and the period of prescription starts to run from the beginning again. Pursuant to the Civil Code, the lapse of the period of prescription occurs:

- if the right was granted by an effective court decision or another authority;
- if the right was acknowledged by the debtor in writing as for the grounds and the amount.

In both cases, a ten-year period of limitation is applied.

The most serious difficulties are in distinguishing an interruption and a suspension of the period of prescription. If an interruption occurs, the period of prescription is not running, but after removing the obstacle the periods of prescription, that is, the periods before and after the obstacle are added up. With a suspension of the time limit, the time lapsed is not taken into consideration, and after removing the obstacle the period of prescription starts to run again from the beginning.

§2. Interpretation

62. A juridical act is interpreted whenever applied and whenever it is necessary. The purpose of the interpretation is to establish the will of the acting person expressed in the content of the juridical act. The interpretation then ascertains the existence of real consequences of a juridical act, that is, formation, changes or termination of legal relationships, or rights and obligations.

Usually the content of a juridical act is ascertained from the verbal form of the juridical act. This, however, does not always provide an unambiguous path to ascertain the real content of will manifestation; therefore, other circumstances in which the will manifestation was presented must be also taken into consideration. The content cannot be derived merely from the name of a juridical act.

An interpretation of a juridical act is done by the acting persons themselves mainly in exercising the rights arising from it, or by the respective state authorities, especially the courts that decide about the exercised rights.

For interpretation of juridical acts and legal provisions, the same legal rules are generally applied. This principle applies mainly to sets of particular interpretation methods (see jurisprudence texts).

In interpretations of juridical acts, special attention should be paid to unification of results of all manners and methods of interpretation. Particular aspects of the content interpretation of a single juridical act and all respective aspects in their mutual links should be understood within this framework. Acts expressed in words should be interpreted not only consistently with their expressing in the language but also consistently with the will of the person who carried out the respective juridical act unless this will is contrary to the verbal expression. Juridical acts expressed in another manner are interpreted consistently with what the manner of their expression commonly means. The will of the acting person is considered and the good faith of the person to whom the juridical act was directed is protected.

§3. Conditional Contracts

63. The contractual terms regulating a right or obligation may provide that it is provided upon the occurrence of an event of which the parties do not know that it may occur at all, or an event that certainly will occur, but the parties do not know when, or a past event that the parties are unaware of.

The condition may involve an objective fact (e.g., reaching an age) or a subjective fact (concluding a contract).

The purpose of the condition enables the party to carry out a juridical act also at the time when not all facts are known that will be involved when the juridical act will be carried out. This applies in the instance when both the rise and the termination of legal consequences are tied to the fulfilment of the condition.

Conditions must be objectively possible and allowed. A condition must be objectively possible, that is, there must be a possibility to carry it out. Physical objective impossibility of a suspensive condition results in invalidity of a juridical act in respect of annulling the condition (invalidity of the condition as a whole or partially); objective impossibility of resolutive condition results in invalidity of the condition (the condition is disregarded).

Condition is admissible if it is not contrary to law, may not evade law or is not inconsistent with good morals. An inadmissible condition should result in invalidity of the juridical act or a condition. However, Slovak courts respect the autonomy of will of the parties.[9]

In the Slovak law, conditions are classified according to various criteria, one of the most significant being dependence of the juridical act effectiveness upon the fulfilment of a condition. Therefore, conditions are divided into suspensive and resolutive. Suspensive conditions are linked with effectiveness of a juridical act in such a manner that the juridical act made dependent on such a condition takes effect

9. Cf. the ruling of the Supreme Court R 57/1999: 'A suspensive condition in a contract of sale in accordance with the Commercial Code consisting in that the buyer will pay the sale price within a certain period after it being paid by another buyer is not an impossible condition that is disregarded.'

upon the fulfilment of the condition at the time when the juridical act exists as valid but is not effective. After fulfilment of the suspensive condition, the juridical act becomes effective as a rule since the condition has been fulfilled. The juridical act does not take effect if fulfilment of the condition was intentionally caused by the party obtaining benefit from it even though he was not supposed to cause it. In such a case, fulfilment of the condition is regarded as not executed. The ultimate impossibility to fulfil the condition results in the final decision that the juridical act will not take effect in the future, either, and the same consequences occur due to prevention of the condition fulfilment, that is, rendering fulfilment impossible through some kind of interference. If the fulfilment of the condition was intentionally prevented by the party gaining benefit from that, the juridical act becomes unconditional. Resolutive conditions take effect in such a manner that by fulfilling them the effect (relevant right or obligation) of a juridical act comes to an end. This means that the juridical act was effective but upon fulfilment of a resolutive condition the effectiveness expires. Before the condition was resolved, a state of uncertainty had existed based on the question whether the juridical act may become ineffective or not. By fulfilling the resolutive condition the effect of a juridical act expired, as a rule upon the instant of its fulfilment with the effect *ex nunc*. A juridical act does not become ineffective if the fulfilment of the condition was caused intentionally by the party who benefited from it but the party was not supposed to cause it. Finally, the decision that the condition cannot be fulfilled results in the juridical act to continue and ceases to be conditional. Preventing the fulfilment of a resolutive condition has the same effect; only in the case when the fulfilment of the condition was prevented intentionally by the party benefiting from it, the juridical act becomes unconditional.

Another criterion for the conditions classification is the nature of conditions. Therefore we distinguish positive conditions (depending on whether a certain situation will occur, has occurred or exists), and a negative condition (depending on whether certain situation will not occur, has not occurred or does not exist).

From the viewpoint of the party influencing a condition to occur, we may distinguish the conditions that can be fulfilled (potestative), accidental (causal) conditions, and mixed conditions. Potestative conditions are those the content of which is a fact that can be performed by the party. It means that their fulfilment or failure to fulfil can be influenced by human will. Fulfilment of accidental conditions is out of human will. Thus fulfilling these conditions depends on circumstances that are not under the control of persons.

Chapter 4. Privity of Contract

§1. The Rule of Privity of Contract

64. The Slovak law of contract is based (in addition to the principle of contract autonomy) on equality of the parties to the contract. This means that:

> either party may not one-sidedly impose his will on the other party, and either party may not one-sidedly decide in his own dispute (nemo est index in propria causa).

I. Third Parties and the Contract

65. The principle of equality mentioned above means that a third party is not bound by agreements of contract parties, the exceptions being the cases established by law or the cases when the third party joins actively the contractual relationship concluded between other parties.

II. Contract for the Benefit of a Third Party

66. An initial requirement of equality of parties prevents third parties from being affected by contractual agreement. However, the Slovak law of contract admits to conclude a contract for the benefit of a third party, the effects of such contract being bound to the consent of third party.

Obligations for the benefit of a third party arise upon a contract by which the debtor (prominent) is obliged to the creditor (provisor) to perform upon the contract relation to the third party (tertius). The tertius will not participate actively in this contract relation. The tertius becomes a creditor, entitled to demand performance, at the moment when he has manifested his will in a legally relevant form to accept the performance (the form of will manifestation is not prescribed, it may only be implied). If a third party was to accept a performance without his consent, it would be violation of a civil law principle under §2, paragraph 2 on equality of parties. At the moment, the tertius manifests the will to accept the performance arising from the contract he takes part in the creditor's rights with all objections available to the creditor. It is therefore immaterial whether the creditor has had these (subjective) objections and intended to exercise them, or he might have been unaware of them, or he could not or did not want to exercise them. The debtor also retains all objections he might have against the creditor. Pursuant to the same provision of the Civil Code, the creditor himself may claim performance, unless agreed otherwise. If the tertius refuses to accept the performance, the promisor is entitled to demand performance but only if so agreed in advance. If the tertius refuses his consent to the performance arising from the contract, the promisor is entitled to demand the performance, unless agreed otherwise.

Any contract may be concluded for the benefit of a third party unless it is inconsistent with its nature, that is, it is inconsistent with law, evades law, or is inconsistent with good morals. Typically, such contracts are included in the Civil Code as, for example, insuring third parties, or vouchers etc.

Obligations for the benefit (but also to the debt) of third parties must always be distinguished from agency. For these obligations, a third person is a party to the contract whereas the agent is not.

III. Contract to the Debit of a Third Party

67. The Civil Code does not recognize obligations to the debit of third parties because they present a principal violation of civil regulation of equality of parties by the fact that one party obliges the other that is not a party to the contract for the benefit of the creditor. The concept of obligations to the debit of third parties is not acceptable in this pure form. Contractual obligation cannot arise to a person who himself is not a party to the contract. Therefore, parties to the contract may only agree on the so-called promise of intercession of the debtor with a third party to provide performance. Then it is the breach of promise of intercession of the debtor with the third party that will be deemed as a breach of obligation, not failure to perform by the third party for the benefit of the creditor.

§2. Transfer of Contractual Rights and/or Obligations

I. The Term and Kinds of Changes in Obligations

68. It is socially desirable to enable one or more elements of the structure of contract relations to undergo certain changes while they endure. In some cases, a change may be deemed so principal that the changed obligation is required by law to be deemed a new obligation. In other cases, the current obligation, upon undergoing changes, has retained characteristic features of the original obligation to such an extent that it is not considered as a new contract but merely as an altered contract.

Changes in contracts may arise only if during the existence of the original obligation certain legal situation arises that is prescribed by law as a change of certain terms only. The alteration of contract may be performed under an agreement of the parties or a unilateral juridical act, an official ruling, or an illegal conduct of a person (delay). Legal grounds for a change of an obligation are the original legal situation along with a new situation causing the obligation to change.

Contract relations are usually classified according to which contract element is involved in the change. These changes are classified as:

- changes involving the parties;

– changes in the content and subject matter of an obligation.

Changes in the content and subject matter of an obligation are included in one category because a change in the subject matter causes in turn a change in single rights and obligations of the parties.

(For more about changes in the content, *see* above in the Chapter 1, §1, IV. Modifications).

The Slovak law recognizes the following kinds of changes involving the parties:

(a) assignment of a claim (*cessio*);
(b) assumption of debt – substitution of a new debtor;
(c) accession to an obligation – adhesion to liability for debt;
(d) agreement to perform through a third person – voucher (assignatio) and instrument (voucher) for performance in securities;
(e) transfer of contractual position.

a. Assignment of a Claim
The Term and the Rise of the Legal Relationship

69. Assignment of a claim is such an alteration of obligation where, based on a certain legal situation (most frequently a contract between a debtor and a creditor), a new creditor, also called a cessionary or assignee, replaces the previous creditor, also called assignor, in the relationship while the original relationship continues to exist.

As for this type of change regulated under Slovak law, we distinguish an assignment of a claim established by the agreement of the parties (*cessio voluntaria*) and an assignment of a claim independent of the will of the parties (*cessio necessaria*, forced assignment of claim), which can be either a statutory assignment of a claim (*cessio ex lege*) arising directly from rules of law, and an assignment of a claim arising from a court decision (*cessio judicaria*). While statutory assignment of a claim is stipulated for particular situations in various legal provisions (e.g., providing performance to the creditor by the guarantor under the surety on behalf of the debtor) and the same applies to the change of the creditor based on a court decision (a number of such instances are stipulated under the Civil Procedure, for example, enforcement of judgment by ordering a claim), general provisions of contract law under the Civil Code concern contractual assignment of the rights.

Voluntary assignment of the rights arises by a written contract based on which previous creditor, the assignor, transfers his claim upon a new creditor, the cessionary.

The debtor is excluded from the procedure as under law his consent to the transfer of the claim is deemed unnecessary for the claim transfer to be valid as the debtor's situation undergoes no change by the claim transfer.[10] Regarding the obligatory nature of the claim transferred, the Civil Code stipulates instances where a claim cannot be transferred. Such claims are excluded due to their nature, which become extinct no later than upon the creditor's death (e.g., the right to recover compensation for injuries

10. *See* ruling 2 Cdo 36/2003.

and for a difficult social position and assertion), claims the content of which would change upon the change of the creditor (e.g., an obligation to teach music) and claims not enabling legal recourse through enforcement. Besides, the possibility of an assignment of a claim may be excluded in advance by an agreement of the creditor and the debtor (§525, paragraph 2).

Content of Legal Relationship

70. The content of an assignment of a claim, that is, mutual rights and obligations between the parties, will differ according to whether the claim has been ceded for money or gratuitously. In the case of an assignment of a claim subject to payment, the assignor is liable to the cessionary where:

- the claim was not assigned to cessionary with the content agreed;
- the debtor has performed the obligation to the assignor before the assignment of the claim;
- the claim ceded or its part became extinct by setting off the debtor's claim to the assignor.

The assignor is liable for the claim recoverability only if so stipulated expressly by a contract, and only up to the amount of the claim obtained along with ancillary rights. The assignor's liability, as stated above, is absent, if the assignor has not claimed the debt ceded in court without an unnecessary delay.

Contrary to that, if the claim has been ceded gratuitously, the assignor, as may be deduced from the arguments given in the provisions mentioned above, has no such liability.

At the instant of the assignment of claim, the assignor forfeits the claim and the right to performance that is obtained by the cessionary.[11] The condition is that the debtor must be notified about the assignment of the claim, that is, the duty to notify rests on the assignor. However, regarding the written form of the agreement on an assignment of a claim, it is also possible for the cessionary to notify but in a satisfactory manner (e.g., by submitting the written text of the contract). Before the debtor has been notified about the claim ceded, he may perform for the benefit of the assignor or to settle the claim otherwise with him. The assignor is bound to hand over to the cessionary and transfer upon him all legal remedies and security tools concerning the ceded claim and to give him all the necessary information.

The necessity to protect creditor's rights has led to the provision that even after the assignment of a claim the debtor keeps all defences (remedies) he had against the initial creditor at the time of the assignment of the claim. Moreover, the debtor may

11. The assignor's relevant notification of the debtor about the assignment of debt entitles the cessionary to demand the assigned debt. Courts take such a notification into consideration without examining as a pre-judicial question whether the contract of assignment existed or was valid. In such a case, the debtor cannot successfully claim invalidity of the contract of assignment or its non-existence. He could do that if the assignment of debt was claimed by the cessionary showing a contract of assignment. (*See* ruling 4 Obo 210/2001).

claim his objections against the assignor and also against the cessionary, even though they have not yet been matured at the time of the assignment of the claim.

With the ceded claim, all its supplements are transferred to the cessionary. The assignor and the cessionary may also agree that the supplements of the claim remain with the assignor.[12]

If the ceded claim has been secured by a surety, the assignor is bound to notify the person who provided the surety about the assignment of the claim.

Even if a claim has been effectively ceded the assignor may, when demanded by the cessionary, claim the debt from the debtor at the cessionary's cost. If the debtor has been notified about the assignment of the claim, such a debt may be claimed only if it is not claimed by the cessionary himself and the assignor passes the cessionary's consent to the debtor.

Assumption of Debt: Substitution of a New Debtor

The Term and the Origin

71. An assumption of a debt arises when a new debtor joins the existing obligation relationship instead of the current debtor.

A true assumption of a debt probably arises only in cases presuming it upon an agreement between the debtor and the third party with the creditor's consent.[13]

However, the Civil Code regulates situations where the third party has agreed with the creditor to take over the debt without an agreement with the debtor. Transfer of liabilities upon the third party is inconsistent with the civil law principles. In such a case, the law does not specify performance of mutual relationship in liabilities.

A mandatory written form is required by law in such a case. Even though the content of obligation basically does not change by the debt assumption, the surety provided by the third party is preserved only if this person has expressed his consent to the debt assumption. Besides, a major part of the claim surety becomes extinct, due to the nature of the matter (exceptions may be material sureties) as it is bound to the person of the debtor and upon changing the debtor it has no sense (e.g., an agreement on wage deductions, etc.). To secure the position of the creditor, it may be held that the claim surety provided by acknowledgement of the original debtor (§558) is effective also for the new debtor.

The Content of Legal Relationship

12. *See* ruling Obpj 2/1999.
13. The consent of the creditor in the sense of §531, para. 1, Civil Code, may be granted either in advance or additionally, and the law does not establish any formal requirements for such an act. It is a unilateral act which may be written, oral or even implied (ruling 5 Obo 167/2001).

The creditor who was informed by the debtor that his debt has been taken over by another person does not have a duty to notify the debtor about his disagreement with the debt being taken over. If the creditor remains passive after such information, it cannot be considered as his consent to the debt being taken over. The consent may be made in any manner that does not give rise to doubts whether the creditor agrees with the debt being taken over (ruling 4 Obo 138/1995).

72. Being there a valid assumption of the debt, the new debtor is bound to perform instead of the original debtor and the creditor is entitled to claim the performance from him. Even without an express stipulation by law, it is presumed that the content of obligation has not changed upon the debt assumption and thus the new debtor has all defences available as the original debtor had to assert them against the creditor, except the manifestation directed to set off the claim of the original debtor towards the creditor. There are no mutual claims of the creditor and the new debtor and thus setting off is implicitly excluded, as the original debtor has withdrawn from the debt.

If only a part of the debt is taken over on the basis of a contract for assumption of debt, the duty to pay the supplements, existing on the day when the debt is taken over, is not transferred to the new debtor.[14]

If a contract of a debt (obligation) assumption has been made between debtors but the creditor either did not consent to or refused his consent to the debt assumption, such a contract is effective under law only in relation to the original debtor and the new debtor, but does not have legal effects for the creditor, who is entitled to demand performance from the original debtor and to refuse accepting performance from another party. Therefore, the new debtor would have to give, under such a contract, performance to the original debtor, who will in turn give this performance to the creditor.

Accession to an Obligation: Adhesion to Liability for Debt

The Term and the Origin of the Legal Relationship

73. Accession to debt is such a type of a change of the contractual relationship when a third party joins the current creditor and obliges himself to perform his monetary obligation on his behalf. In this case, adhesion to the obligation is effective without an agreement with the creditor.

However, if a third party agrees with the debtor to pay his debt to the creditor, he thus obliges himself to the debtor to perform for his creditor. The creditor who is not a party to such an obligation is not directly entitled to demand performance from the third party – the new debtor.

The Content of Legal Relationship

74. Following an effective accession to a debt obligation, the creditor may demand performance both from the original and from the new debtor, or from both. Regarding the possible wording of the statement of claim (as a rule, the creditor is entitled to sue both co-debtors simultaneously for performance to be provided jointly and severally), a relation of passive solidarity arises. This, however, applies only to the relationship of co-debtors towards the creditor. Under law, no recourse relationship arises between the debtors after one of them has duly performed. It could be taken into consideration only if solidarity relationship was agreed between co-debtors in advance. By performing the debt by one of the debtors, the obligation of the other to perform becomes extinct, too. Unless the original debtor wishes to be bound by the

14. *See* ruling 1 Obdo 17/2002 (R 5/2004).

new debtor as a result of the debt performing (based on inner relationship between the co-debtors), he should precede the cessionary in performing.

After concluding such an agreement, the new debtor is obliged to the previous debtor, for whom a right to demand performance by the new debtor for himself arises directly towards the creditor. No direct titles or duties arise to the creditor under this obligation.

Agreement to Perform Through a Third Person: Voucher (*assignatio*) and Instrument – Voucher for Performance in Securities

75. This agreement is called 'voucher' – *assignatio* – in the Slovak law. The holder of voucher is entitled to obtain performance from a third party (remittor) who is authorized to perform for the voucher holder on the account of the remitter. A voucher is a compound obligation relationship under law which, even if classified among changed obligations, is aimed to perform through a third party.

A voucher is composed of three basic relationships, arising among three different parties. The parties are: the creditor (assignee), the debtor (assignor), and a third party performing for the assignor. The respective relationships arising within a voucher are:

- Relationship of value, expressing as a rule the basic value of the relationship as a whole, which is the value of performance between the creditor and the debtor. This relationship arises through conclusion of agreement between an assignor and an assignee, under which the assignor's debt will be performed by accepting performance from the third party.
- Relationship of remittance (payment) arises by authorizing the third party by the assignor to perform to the assignee. Two variants are possible here: if the third party is bound to the assignor to accept the voucher (e.g., based on a contract of current account or of credit already made), he is bound to accept the voucher. If there is no such relationship, an agreement on accepting the voucher must be made between the assignor and the third party.
- Relationship of payment arises by accepting the voucher by the third party and notifying the assignee about accepting the voucher. By this act, the assignee obtains a direct right to performance provided by the third party.

Voucher is a general type of an obligation change and has no prescribed form in neither of the juridical acts in which it arises and is executed.

As for the nature of performance, voucher is an obligation with a vicarious performance.

As it is a three-sided relationship, causing the risk of imbalance in legal relationships of the parties, these relationships are regulated by law in such a manner as to allow conditions for its balance.

An important reference to the appropriate application of the provision on the contract of mandate if the parties did not agree otherwise is contained under.

Voucher may be cancelled only by the time it has been accepted by the third party.

A special form of a voucher regarding a security warrant is provided by the Civil Code. These are abstract obligations where the cause need not be stated. If the warrant bears the claimant's name, it can be transferred by endorsement by which all rights arising from the warrant are transferred to the entitled person based on the endorsement.

The person who has accepted a voucher issued by a monetary institution is bound to perform for the person for whose benefit the voucher was issued or transferred under.

More detailed provisions describe regulations of bills of exchange and cheques.

Transfer of Contractual Position

76. Transfer of the whole contractual position of a party to a third person is not known in Slovak law as a specific (named) type of transfer of rights and obligations. For such a purpose, an unnamed contract (*contractus innominatus*) can be used.

§3. The Special Case of a Sub-contract, For Example the (Nominated) Sub-contractor in Building Contracts

77. Slovak Contract Law does not specify a sub-contract. However, the terms 'sub-contract' and 'sub-contractor' are used, especially in building contracts. These contracts are not expressly stipulated by law and thus it is up to the parties' will to define its content. One of the few exceptions is a mutual tie of guaranty periods in the principal contract and the sub-contract, under which the guaranty under sub-contracts may not lapse before the guaranty concerning the subject matter of this sub-contract under the principal contract.

§4. Actio Pauliana

78. The Roman *actio pauliana* is applied under the Slovak Civil Code to the institute of contesting (raising objections to demand relative ineffectiveness of the juridical act).

Actio Pauliana is based on the option to claim ineffectiveness of legal consequences towards a particular person only pursuant to 42a and 42b, Slovak Civil Code. The creditor may demand that the Court determine that the debtor's juridical acts, if reducing his own recoverable[15] claims (enforceability is not necessary), are ineffective.[16] It is possible to raise objections against juridical acts performed by the debtor in the past three years with the intent to reduce enforceability of the creditor's claim, were the other party aware of the intention or the juridical acts between the debtor and persons close to him, except for the instances where the other party was then unable, even

15. The legal concept of 'recoverable claim' covers such a claim that can be successfully demanded in court in the trial proceedings (R 44/2001).
16. The person who acquires from a debtor title to a thing does not lose it even in the case when the creditor has successfully brought *Actio Pauliana* against the legal act of the debtor (R 88/2001).

though exercising due care, to recognize the debtor's intent to reduce the enforceability of the creditor's claim. The creditor's success in raising an objection results in the option for the creditor to demand the debt be satisfied from the part by which the debtor's property was reduced through the objected juridical act. If this is impossible (e.g., the subject matter of performance has become extinct or transferred to another party), the creditor may claim recovery from the party which obtained benefit from the objected juridical act.[17]

17. The creditor who successfully contested a legal act pursuant to §42a, Civil Code is entitled to monetary compensation from the person who benefited from that act and the thing acquired by that act is not with him (R 110/1998).

Chapter 5. Termination of a Contract

79. The particular manners of termination of an obligation can be classified according to various criteria.

With regard to whether upon termination of an obligation also creditor's debt has been discharged, we distinguish obligations as:

(a) obligations with the creditor satisfied (*cum satisfactione creditoris*) which are for example, performance, novation, or settlement;
(b) obligations without the creditor satisfied (sine satisfactione creditoris) which are for example, withdrawal from the contract, impossibility, or waiver of a right.

Under the Slovak law, termination of a contract can be made in the following ways:

- §1. Debt Fulfilment: Performance and Breach.
- §2. Impossibility and Hardship: Unforeseen Impossibility.
- §3. Withdrawal from the Contract.
- §4. Setting off (Unilateral and by Agreement).
- §5. Agreement on a New Obligation (Novation).
- §6. Waiver of a Right.
- §7. Remission of a Debt.
- §8. Settlement.
- §9. Lapse of Time.
- §10. Death of the Debtor or the Creditor.
- §11. Preclusion of Rights.
- §12. Debtors Delay under 'Fixed' Contract.
- §13. Merger of Debts.

§1. Debt Fulfilment: Performance and Breach

80. Performance is a juridical act by which the debtor (or a third party, the surety, etc.) gives performance to the creditor who accepts this performance (it is not a bilateral juridical act). Mutual consent of the parties is not necessary – this is basically given in a juridical act itself, giving rise to the obligation, and in law governing rules for performing an obligation. For example, a debtor can perform even without the creditor's cooperation by placing a thing in an official deposit, and this act will be deemed as performance, although the respective creditor's act will be missing in this case.

The essentials of performance of a contractual obligation are:

(a) existence of an obligation;
(b) unilateral act of the debtor, directed to provide performance;
(c) unilateral act of the creditor, who accepts the performance.

Parties to performance are as a rule identical to the parties to the obligation.

On the debtor side, it is mostly the debtor himself; this is explicitly stated by law for the obligations. The subject matter is performance that must be provided by the debtor in person, as performance by a third person would be of a different quality. Performance, however, may be provided also by a third person who is bound to perform either under law, by an official ruling or under a contract. Thus, the surety will be bound to provide performance if the debtor has not performed his debt upon the call of the creditor (e.g., a salary payer who has not complied with the contract of payroll deduction, a spouse performing on behalf of the other spouse, if it is the case of community property of spouses, performance provided by an agent, etc). Recourse between the party who performed instead of the debtor and the debtor is possible only if stipulated by law. Performance provided by the third person should be based on specific legal grounds. If there are no grounds, such performance establishes the relationship of unjustified enrichment and a duty of the benefiting person to return the performance.

On the creditor's side, principally it is the creditor, who is entitled to accept performance (the duty to provide performance to the creditor in person is stipulated under law, but it may also be a person different from the creditor).

Such cases occur most frequently if:

(a) the creditor must have a statutory representative due to his incapability to carry out the particular juridical act (taking over performance), the debtor is bound to perform into the hands of the statutory representative in order to discharge his duty;
(b) the creditor will authorize an attorney to take over the performance;
(c) in assignment of claim by the time the debtor has been duly informed about the assignment of claim;
(d) the debtor performs for the person who will present the creditor's voucher on debt receipt, presuming that the debtor acts bona fide. In this case, the debtor can refuse to perform for the person who submitted the creditor's voucher of receipt only if it is a person different from the creditor.

Subject matter of performance can be determined either individually, or just by generic signs, stating that one of the parties (the debtor, unless stated otherwise) will make the selection of the particular things for performance (concentration).

In some cases, unity of performance is required. However, in certain cases performance in part (partial performance) is allowed by law:

- The debtor is bound to perform the obligation all at once only if so expressly agreed; if nothing is agreed in this sense, the debtor must pay the debt all at once only if it were contrary to the nature of the debt by the proof of the contrary.
- Except for the cases stated under the debtor may provide also a partial performance and the creditor is bound to accept it.
- Performance by instalments may be provided by the debtor, if so agreed with the creditor.

The agreement presumes the deadlines agreed in advance and the amount of the instalments.

If the debtor is supposed to perform several debts for the same creditor and the performance is insufficient to cover them all, it is up to the will of the debtor to denote the debt for which the performance is intended as appropriate; if he fails to do so, the performance is appropriate for that debt which is due or is the first one to fall due. In the case of monetary obligation, the performance is to be appropriate first for interests.

The subject of performance must be identical with the subject matter of the obligation (indirect). The creditor is not bound, with some exceptions (e.g., *alternativa facultas*), to accept another performance, such performance is not deemed duly provided and results in the debtor's delay. Another exception to be mentioned is a possibility to conclude a contract during the time of performance, under which the debtor provides a different performance from that originally stated and the creditor accepts it. This institute, called traditionally *datio in solutum*, that is, giving instead of performance, is not expressly stipulated by the Civil Code and could be established by an atypical contract. Different is the case of *datio solutionis causa*, that is, giving for the purpose of performance. Here the debtor transfers a certain thing or a right upon the creditor to satisfy the creditor not through the thing or the right itself (its usable value as a rule) but through its realization (e.g., through sale of the thing and obtaining the sale price, that is, realizing its value). Under this contract, the debt has been discharged upon the moment of value realization of the substitute performance.

The time of performance is stipulated by Civil Code in general. Under the Civil Code, the following principles can be enumerated for determining time of performance:

- Determination of time of performance is principally left up to the parties.
- It is possible under law to leave the time of performance to be fixed by the debtor. If the debtor will not determine the time of performance the creditor may any time ask the court to determine it in consistency with good morals (good faith and fair dealing).
- In the cases of an increased interest in timely and accurate performance, time of performance is regulated by law.
- If time of performance has not been agreed on, regulated by law or determined by court ruling, the debtor is bound to fulfil the debt on the first day after he was so required by the creditor.
- If the time of performance is stipulated mandatorily by a legal regulation, the parties to the contractual relationship are bound by that. If the creditor does not agree with an earlier performance and refuses it, the debt of the debtor does not terminate.[18]

The Commercial Code has put into its text some specific rules about the time of performance, dependent on the procedure of the invoicing and some specific rules applicable for the debtor, being a entity of Public Law (*see* § 340a, 340b, Commercial Code).

18. *See* ruling 1 Cdo 97/1997.

In the case of incompliance with time of performance, the debtor (or the creditor, in respect to cooperation in performing) is in default, legal consequences of which have been described above.

Place of performance is defined as follows: A debt must be performed at the place determined by the parties' agreement. If the place of performance has not been agreed on, the place of performance will be the residence of the debtor. In performing a monetary debt by mail or through a financial institution, the debt is deemed to be paid up at the instant of remitting the respective amount but the parties may agree otherwise, too.

Consequences of Performance

81. Performance results in discharge of the obligation. Other legal consequences are: extinction of surety relations as an ancillary relation and the rise of the duty of the creditor to release to the debtor a receipt of debt fulfilment. If the performance was provided by a surety, a mutual recourse relationship arises between the surety and the debtor. Finally, as an expression of a functional synallagma, the right to demand performance from the other party arises for the party that has fulfilled its debt in mutual claims.

Breach of Contract

82. Obligations must be performed properly and on time. If one of these conditions has not been met, a situation called 'delay' occurs under the Slovak law. Consequences of delay as a breach of contract are described in Chapter 4, §2.

§2. Impossibility and Hardship: Unforeseen Impossibility

83. Debtor's duty to perform terminates when performance becomes impossible. Impossibility of performance is an objectively assessed impossibility, that is, not an impossibility based merely on the debtor's belief in impossibility to provide performance as required. Economic impossibility (hardship) does not fall within this category. Economic impossibility (hardship) is given if:

- an obligation can be fulfilled only in more difficult conditions or the cost of performance has increased;
- obligation can be fulfilled only after some time of performance.

It arises from the nature of things that performance may become impossible on the basis of merely individual assessment. Generic performance can be, if of extinction or destruction, or non-attainability, replaced by another performance and does not cause obligation extinction. If only a partial impossibility occurs, the performance terminates only for this part; however, the creditor is entitled to withdraw from the contract, as far as the rest of performance is concerned. In case of partial impossibility, the respective part of obligation terminates. However, contractual relationship terminates as a whole, if from the nature of contract or the purpose of performance, which was known to the parties at the time of the rise of the obligation, derives that the remaining part of obligation has lost economic value for the creditor, unless the creditor has informed the debtor without a delay that he insists on the rest of the performance being provided.

§3. Withdrawal from the Contract

84. Under Slovak law, it is possible to avoid an obligation by withdrawal from the contract.

In some situations, it is not possible to insist justifiably on strict adherence to the contract *(pacta sunt servanda).* An important interest of those involved in civil relations led to adopting some exceptions to the principle as stated above. One of the exceptions is the option to withdraw from the contract under the Civil Code. Besides, the creditor is entitled to withdraw from a contract under general provisions on obligations under the Civil Code in case of debtor's delay when an additional time fixed by the creditor for the debtor to perform has lapsed (§517, paragraph 1). In addition to this, there are other reasons for withdrawal from a contract contained in the Civil Code, involving partial impossibility to perform, unless this concerns the part of performance that has not become extinct as a result of impossibility of performance. Other options enabling withdrawal are stipulated for specific obligation relationships stated under the Civil Code.

Upon withdrawal, the rights and duties arising from the obligation terminate *ex tunc* (from the very beginning, which means that:

- the debtor is no more bound to pay;
- parties are bound to return to one another the performance already provided;
- right to compensation for damage accrues to the creditor, but only up to the amount, to which the damage is not covered by possible interests of delay, fees of delay or penalization agreed under the contract (liquidation damages).

§4. Setting Off (Unilateral and by Agreement)

85. Unilateral settlement is a unilateral juridical act by which a party sets off its *mutual* debt against the creditor's claim. The obligation has been discharged at the moment when the mutual debts meet which occurs at the instant when the last debt has matured. The conditions of one-sided set off are as follows:

- It must be a type of debt for which setting off is admissible. Setting off against claims involving compensation for bodily or mental harm is excluded unless both debts are of the same kind. The same applies against debts for which enforcement of judgment is not possible. Special provisions allowing setting off against debts in maintenance claims are included in the Family Code.

- It must be a kind of debt that may be set off. Deposit debts and debts not recoverable by court (natural obligations) cannot be set off. Setting off a debt not mature against the debt already mature is not possible, either.

Performance of mutual debts must be of the same kind (e.g., mutual monetary debts). By setting off the debts that cover one another, they become extinct.

Setting off by an agreement arises upon a creditor–debtor agreement, by which the parties set off their mutual debts in accordance with the conditions set by law. Setting off by an agreement has the same legal ground as setting off with the exceptions as follows:

- Setting off by an agreement presumes mutual consent of the parties, also mutual debts, excluded from unilateral setting off may be set off by an agreement. Only the debts involving maintenance paid to minor children are excluded from setting off by an agreement under Family Code.
- Legal consequences of obligation termination by setting off as a rule do not arise upon an effective agreement made, but upon the instant when the mutual debts meet.

In addition, an obligation to perform upon a contract may become extinct as a result of an objective situation such as the one that follows.

§5. Agreement on a New Obligation (Novation)

86. While in previous instances one-sided withdrawal from contractual obligation was involved, an agreement may be concluded between the parties, by which the parties absolve one another from the duties arising from the contract and which can include the following:

- An agreement on a new obligation *(novation)* – this manner of obligation discharge is also called a novation of privity that is distinguished from cumulative novation in which the original obligation does not become extinct, persisting along with the new obligation. Therefore, cumulative novation is usually listed among the ways of changing contractual relationships.
- Agreement on a new obligation as a way of an obligation discharge presumes an agreement between the creditor and the debtor. It can be agreed that another obligation can be performed instead of the original obligation, for example, instead of paying monetary debt ceding a respective part of a real property to the creditor for temporary use without the time stated. By making (concluding) an effective agreement of a new obligation, the original obligation between the parties directed to carry out the original performance becomes extinct. Concurrently, a new obligation arises directed to provide the performance as newly agreed on. Unless anything else has been agreed on, surety of the original obligation terminates along with the novation. An exception is the provision involving suretyship, which in relation to privity novation is retained in the original extent only if the surety

has not expressed his consent to continue. In doubts on replacing the original obligation by a new one, the legal rules in favour of doubtless content of the agreement on the new obligation apply, that is, the content of the original agreement becomes extinct only to the extent it has been doubtlessly replaced by the new contract content.

The formalities of the original obligation apply to the agreement of novation. Under the same provision, the written form is necessary for novation of a statute-barred obligation. As a modification of privity novation, the provisions of the Civil Code stipulate the possibility to cancel the original obligation between the parties without replacing it by a new obligation. In this way, also a part of existing obligation may be cancelled.

§6. Waiver of a Right

87. Waiver of right arises by an agreement of the debtor and creditor, on the basis of which the creditor waives his right to demand the whole debt or its part to the debtor. Unlike debt remission, which is of a similar nature, waiver of right is typical for obligations involving non-monetary performance.

The conditions for waiver of rights are:

(a) There is an agreement in writing between the creditor and the debtor. The requirement of a written agreement is given by its significance because it interferes unilaterally with the position of contractual parties.
(b) The creditor may not effectively waive his rights that may arise in the future; only as such an agreement would be sanctioned by invalidity. For example, it is not possible, at the time of purchasing a new product, to waive the right to claim compensation in liability for faulty products within warranty period.
(c) The legal consequence of waiver of right is termination of obligation to the extent stated. Surety of obligation terminates only if the creditor has waived the debt as a whole.

§7. Remission of Debt

88. Remission of debt is a manner similar to termination of an obligation by waiver of a right, which can be seen in stipulating both manners of termination in one provision by attaching the same legal consequences to debt remission and waiver of right.

The difference between remission of debt and waiver of debt is their application. Each of these manners are used for termination of different types of obligations.

Like waiver of right, remission of debt arises upon an agreement of both parties under which the creditor remits the debtor's debt.

If several individuals are included on the debtor's party, the nature of plurality will be decisive. For severable performance, remission of debt will be possible also towards some of the debtors or just one debtor. In non-severable performance that can be fulfilled only by common activities of debtors. It follows that the debt can be remitted only to all debtors simultaneously. In the relationship of passive solidarity, remission of debt towards one of the debtors does not influence existence of the right of recourse among the co-debtors.

Remission of debt has different legal consequences depending on whether it involves the whole performance arising from the obligation or from a single debt or its part. If the whole content of obligation is terminated by remission of debt, the whole obligation terminates, too; otherwise, only one debt or a part of a debt terminates.

The respective agreement to be valid must be made in writing.

§8. Settlement

89. The current obligation can be replaced also in such a manner that the parties settle their mutual rights and obligation, so far questionable, by an agreement.

This agreement, also called *transactio*, is aimed to make up for the current content of the obligation, which was questionable, by new rights and obligations. Thus all rights (the entire content of the obligation relationship), or only some of them, can be settled between the parties. If all the rights are being replaced, only those rights are exempt that the party making the contract could not consider.

Settlement presumes replacement of current obligation by an obligation arising from settlement. Apparently, settlement is close to privity novation, but it may replace only a part of the current obligation content; then it will be close to cumulative novation.

Settlement agreement will be voidable in case of mistaking what is objectionable or doubtful between the parties and this mistake will be caused by fraudulent conduct of one party.

§9. By Lapse of Time

90. A number of rights and obligations arising from obligation relationships become extinct by lapse of time for which they have been limited. An example may be lapse of the lease period. By lapse of time as an objective legal situation either a single right or an obligation, or the entire obligation relationship becomes extinct. Lapse of time as a fact giving ground for termination of rights, duties, or the entire obligation may be fixed by law or by an agreement of the parties.

§10. Death of the Debtor or the Creditor

91. One principle of obligation law is permanence of the obligation in spite of various circumstances influencing either side. Therefore, for the sake of legal certainty, the Civil Code stipulates that a debtor's or a creditor's death does not principally result in the obligation termination and by the death of either of them the rights and obligations are passed to the respective legal successors. The exception is an obligation termination as a result of the death of the debtor, the content of which was a performance to be provided by the debtor in person. This is not exclusively a performance that cannot be provided by another person; the duty to provide performance by the debtor will derive from the content or nature of the obligation relationship. As for creditor's death, the Civil Code stipulates an exception, under which such debts which are restricted to the creditor's person exclusively are not passed on the heir (e.g., claim to recovery for injuries and difficult social position and assertion).

§11. Preclusion of Rights

92. Unlike other ways of termination of obligation, preclusion is established mainly by lapse of time. The termination of rights and duties arising from an obligation is bound upon the cumulative existence of the two prerequisites as follows:

- lapse of time;
- inaction of the entitled party.

§12. Debtor's Delay Under 'Fixed' Contract

93. It may be concluded that termination of contract *ex lege* occurs as a result of cumulative co-existence of the two facts:

- a debtor's delay in a fixed contract, that is, if the contract has stipulated a strict period for performance and it arises from the contract or from the nature of the thing that the creditor has no interest in delayed performance;
- creditor's failure to notify without delay that he insists on performance in spite of the debtor's delay.

§13. Merger of Debts

94. Merger as a reason for termination of obligation may arise due to various legal grounds; therefore, this type is listed separately as a type of termination under §584 of the Civil Code.

A merger of debts arises when the attributes of debtor and creditor are united in the same (natural or legal) person in the same capacity.

Part II. Specific Contracts

95. In explaining the particular contract types and their regulation under the Civil Code, attention is paid to the most important characteristic features of these contracts and to the most distinct feature distinguishing the particular contract from general provisions.

The following text is observed in explaining the particular types of contracts:

- the notion, legal regulation, creation;
- rights and obligations of the parties;
- liability;
- discharge.

If any of these essentials is missing, general provisions apply.

The Slovak regulation of the consumer contracts is explained in the first chapter, in a similar way as regulated in the Slovak Code Civil.

Chapter 1. Consumer Contract: General Provisions

96. According to the EU legislation, consumer contracts involve no specific type of contract. Consumer contracts are contracts where the consumer is in the position of a non-entrepreneur. The Civil Code requires a supplier (the businessman) and a consumer, who are simply and explicitly defined for this purpose, to be the parties to the contract. A supplier is a person (natural person or a company) acting within its business or other entrepreneurial activity. A consumer is a person (a natural person or a company) who, in making and performing the contract, does not act within its business or other entrepreneurial activity.

Consumer contracts are defined under law by examples listed, that is, as contract of purchase, contract for work done, or other contract as provided by the Civil Code. Other contracts explicitly mentioned in the Civil Code are the contract of sale in shops (as a special type of sale contract), contract of mandate, contract of bailment, contract of agency, etc. Further consumer contracts are:

- distance contracts;
- contracts concluded outside usual business facilities.

§1. General Rules for Consumer Contracts

97. General provisions for consumer contracts are contained in §52 and §54, Civil Code.

Contractual agreements involving consumer contracts may not divert from the letter of law to the detriment of the consumer. Consumer protection requires cogency of legal rules where the regulatory cogency is one-sided, more favourable terms may undoubtedly be bargained in favour of the consumer. A consumer may not waive his rights as granted by law, or otherwise weaken his contractual position.

The objective of this norm is to bar consumer contracts from containing a stipulation inconsistent with a bona fide requirement and avoid a significant imbalance of rights and obligations of the parties to the detriment of the consumer. This general clause is specified in the list of unfair terms.

Balanced positions of parties to the contract cannot be understood rigidly. There may exist spheres in legal relations between a consumer and a supplier where it is impossible to demand balance of terms.

The Civil Code contains the following list of unfair terms:

(a) they are supposed to be fulfilled by the consumer and he did not have a chance to learn them before the conclusion of the contract;
(b) they allow the supplier to transfer rights and duties from the contract to another supplier without the consumer's consent, if recoverability of debts or the consumer's claim security has been impaired as a result of the transfer;
(c) they exclude or restrict liability of the supplier for acting or omission by which death or injury of the consumer was caused;

(d) they exclude or restrict rights of the consumer in asserting a claim for product liability or damage liability;
(e) they enable the supplier not to convey the consideration into the hands of the consumer even if the consumer does not make a contract with the supplier or withdraws from it;
(f) they enable the supplier to withdraw from the contract without a contractual or legal reason and the consumer is not enabled to do so;
(g) they enable the supplier to discharge without special reasons a contract made for an indefinite term without a reasonable period of notice;
(h) they order the consumer to perform all obligations even if the supplier has not fulfilled his own obligations as accrued;
(i) they allow the supplier to alter one-sidedly the contractual terms for reasons not stipulated in the contract;
(j) they stipulate that the price of goods or service will be determined at the time of performance, or allow the supplier to raise the price of goods or services without the consumer being entitled to withdraw from the contract, if the price agreed upon at the time of the conclusion of the contract was considerably higher than that at the time of performance;
(k) they require the consumer who has failed to perform his obligation to pay an unreasonably high amount of money as a sanction for not performing his obligation;
(l) they restrict access to evidence or they impose a duty on the consumer to bear the burden of proving that should be borne by a different party to the contract according to the law governing the contractual relationship;
(m) in the case of partial or complete failure to perform an obligation from the part of the supplier they unreasonably restrict or exclude the possibility of the consumer to seek his rights against the supplier including the consumer's right to set off the monetary claim against the supplier;
(n) they have the effect that validity of the contract concluded for a fixed-term is prolonged after the expiry of the term and the consumer is given an unreasonably short time for declaring his consent with the prolonging of the contract;
(o) they entitle the supplier to decide that his consideration is in compliance with the contract or they admit the right to interpret the contract only to the supplier;
(p) they restrict liability of the supplier if the contract was made by an intermediary, or they require the conclusion of the contract by an intermediary in a special manner;
(q) they require in the agreed arbitration clause from the consumer to solve disagreements with the supplier only in an arbitration.

Unfair terms in consumer contracts are invalid.

The Civil Code states an interpretation rule under which, in case of doubts, the interpretation of a contract is more favourable for the consumer. If a contract contains, for example, an expression or stipulation allowing several interpretations, then lack of clarity and thus possible unfavourable consequences will be to the detriment of the supplier. This contract provision of the Civil Code is mandatory, too, and therefore it may not be altered in a consumer contract. This provision is a special legal rule that partially modifies general interpretation rules provided under §35 of the Civil Code. It is based on Article 5, the Council Directive 93/13/EEC.[19]

I. Distance Contracts

98. The legal regulation of the so-called distance contracts (contracts made in distance) reflects the development of the modern means of communication. An essential requirement for conclusion of the contract is to reach contractual accord. The means used by both parties to express their will and thus conclude the contract recognizable by third parties are not restricted in general. Therefore, there are a number of common tools used in the presence of the persons negotiating (a face-to-face negotiation); there are also a number of means enabling negotiation between absent persons (typically employing postal service). Basically with consumer contracts all means enabling distant communication can be utilized. Special attention is paid to some communication media in the Civil Code due to the fact that through their exploitation a considerable risk of abuse against the consumer arises. Except contracts through letter writing, such means are included here that are operated by a businessman providing as his business activity one or more distance communication means and media, namely, non-addressed prints, addressed prints, type letters, advertising prints with an order print, catalogue, telephone attended by a service, telephone without service (automatic call device, audiotext, radio, videophone, electronic mail, fax, etc.).

The range of contracts in which the stipulations protecting consumers do not apply is defined by various criteria: the subject and character of performance, the ways and means used in contracting. The provision on consumer protection in distance contracting does not extend to the contracts:

- for financial services under special acts of law;
- concluded through vending machines or automated shopping places;
- concluded by distance communication means operators via public telephones;
- concluded for construction or sale of real property or involving other rights to real property except tenancy;
- concluded upon auction;
- for supply of food, drinks or other goods of common consumption delivered by standing suppliers into the consumer's house or residence;
- for accommodation, transport, boarding, free time activities, supposing the supplier provides these performances on the date or at the time stated.

19. From an isolated Slovak case concerning consumer protection: No notice or information about the packaging price does not relieve the seller from the duty he has pursuant to §17, Act No. 634/1992 Coll. on consumer protection as amended by Act No. 137/1998 Z.z., to sell products in hygienically safe packing or to pack them in such packing in the act of selling if required by the nature of products. The expenses for packing material and the packaging of products are borne by the seller (rulings 5 Sž 67/2000 and 5 Sž 68/2000.

As consumers often are insufficiently equipped for using such means and facilities, and in order to check the correctness of the relevant data, the law provides certain measures of protection through:

(1) possibility to exclude the use of such means in distance communication;
(2) imposing a duty to the supplier to provide information as stated;
(3) stipulating the option for a consumer to withdraw from the contract in a statutory period.

(1) Other specifying rules are given for some distance communication means. Such means of distance communication enabling individual acts may be used only when the consumer has not rejected their use. Automatic telephone systems without (human) attendance and faxes may be used only upon previous express consent of the consumer.

(2) The proposition submitted by a distance communication means must contain the necessary information for conclusion of the contract under general contract terms provided by the general part of the Civil Code and fundamental contractual terms as provided in Part 8 of the Civil Code (depending on the type of the contract proposed – for example, the subject and price in the sale contract). This information must be provided in a certain and intelligible manner with regard to good morals and to protection of persons, namely, minors or consumers. The requirement of certainty of information concerns the content, intelligibility being a requirement for their expression. The Civil Code further defines the range of particularly necessary information by dividing it into two groups in relation to the time when it must be given to the consumer.

Preliminary information, that is, the information necessary to be given sufficiently in advance of conclusion of the contract (the form is not stipulated):

- the company and identification number of the supplier, the residence;
- name and main characteristics of goods or services;
- price of goods or services including all fees and charges;
- delivery costs;
- guarantee clause;
- the way of guarantee claiming;
- the way of payment, delivery or performance;
- advice on the right to withdraw;
- cost of distance communication means used;
- time period during which the offer or the price is effective.

After conclusion of the contract using distance communication means, no later than prior to performance the consumer must be given the following information (in writing only):

- the company and the supplier's identification number, the residence;
- information related to the terms and the procedures for claiming the right to withdraw from the contract;
- information related to services provided following the sale and guarantees;

- terms for the contract revocation unless the period of the contract validity is longer than one year.

Breach of duty to inform is sanctioned by the right to withdraw from the contract.

(3) Withdrawal from a contract is a unilateral juridical act made by one of the parties to the contract, which results in termination of the contract. Regarding the fact that withdrawal from a contract means breaking the rule '*pacta sunt servanda*', the withdrawal as a juridical act should comply with the requirements set by the law.

The consumer can withdraw from a contract:

- always in correspondence with most general provision for withdrawal if the consumer's right to withdraw has been agreed upon;
- in all cases of conclusion of a distance contract within a period of seven working days following the performance receiving;
- as a sanction for breach of the duty to inform within three months following the performance receiving, or within seven working days following the proper informing during this three-month period.

The last two instances of the rise of the right to withdraw from the contract are, however, limited. The consumer may not withdraw from contracts:

- for providing services if their performance began, with the consumer's consent, before lapse of a seven working-day period following the performance receiving;
- for goods or services supply, the price of which depends on financial market fluctuations regardless of the supplier's will;
- for goods supplies adjusted according to the consumer's wishes or for his person, as well as for perishable goods, goods that are subject to quick deterioration or aging;
- for supply of audio and video records and computer programs if the consumer breaks their original cover;
- for supply of newspapers, journals and magazines;
- based on games or lottery.

Related to provisions for distance contracts, consequences the Civil Code contains are also an explicit formulation of the so-called habitual sale. In accepting the proposition to conclude a contract the principle '*qui tacit, consentire videtur*' does not apply although acceptance may be evolved from an implied expression of will. If the supplier delivers the performance to the consumer without any order, the consumer is not bound to provide consideration to the supplier or even let him know about it (this is no case of unjustified enrichment).

II. Contracts Negotiated Away from Business Premises

99. These are contracts concluded outside the spaces usual for the supplier's operation or anywhere else if the businessman has no permanent place to operate (e.g., peddling). Consumer protection is based on his right to rescind the contract within various periods of time, the length of which is dependent on performing the goods or service delivery by the supplier and possibly on violation of the duty to inform. No later than following the conclusion of contract the supplier is obliged to notify in writing the consumer about his right to withdraw from the contract. The written notification must state also the name of person including his residence with whom this right must be claimed.

The consumer is entitled to withdraw from the contract:

- in the period of seven working days after conclusion of the contract;
- in the period of one month after conclusion of the contract unless goods or service delivery by the supplier has been performed.

Consumer protection may be performed for all contracts concluded outside operation facilities, except:

- the contracts for whose the consumer explicitly arranged the supplier's visit to make an order;
- contracts the purpose of which is a construction, sale, lease or other right to land except for the contracts for their reconstructions, and for deliveries of equipment making part of them;
- contracts for supply of foods or other goods of common consumption delivered by standing suppliers to consumer's household or to other place denoted by him;
- contracts for delivery of goods or services according to the supplier's catalogue that the consumer could learn about in the absence of the supplier, providing that the contact between the parties is to continue in performing a contract as made or any other contract, and providing that the consumer may rescind the contract within at least seven days following the goods takeover and that he is notified of this right by the catalogue or by the contract;
- insurance contracts and securities contracts.

There has been registered, since 2014, in the frame of 'civil' consumer protection, the noticeable development. Some new legal acts make the consumer protection stronger.

Act No. 102/2014 Coll.

100. Mentioned act gives the protection to the consumers when buying the goods or providing the services based on the distance contract or on the contract concluded out of business promises of seller/provider. The aims of this act is the transposition of the Directive of European Parliament and Council 2011/83/EU. To the moment of coming into force of the new legal act, former Act No. 108/2000 Col. has been cancelled.

The Act No. 102/2014 Col. mainly:

- unified the term 'consumer': under the term 'consumer' are newly understood only the physical persons;

- made wider the list of unfair business practices;
- introduced the prohibition of the use of the bill of exchange and/or check for securing the provider's contractual position against the consumer;
- stated the obligation of courts consider 'ex offo' during the trial, if there exists the prescription of provider's claim against consumer;
- stated the smallest font size of the text of consumer contracts (actually 1.9 mm).

Act No. 106/2014 Coll.

101. Second Act, changing the consumer law, introduced into Slovak contract law the consumer's protection mainly against usurious practices of providers of loans and credits, further gives the larger possibility of withdrawal from the contract etc. Newly the contract enabling the provider's usurious practices is considered to be void. The Act establishes newly the limitation of amount of fees negotiated in the credit or loan consumer contract.

Chapter 2. Sales

§1. 'Civil' Sale

102. Purchase and sale is a legal relationship arising from a contract of sale. One party (the seller) is bound to hand over the subject of sale to the other party (the purchaser) who is bound to take it over and pay the purchase price. Both parties to a contract of purchase may comprise several subjects (e.g., an item is being sold or obtained through the sale by co-owners). The essential terms of a sale contract are a subject matter of sale and sale price:

(a) All things that are things in the legal sense and are in possession of the seller but are not *extra commercium* (e.g., things in exclusive possession of the state) can be subject to sale contract. The object of sale contract may be determined individually, in kind, in bulk, or in total. The object of sale contract need not exist at the time of conclusion of the contract; sale of a future thing may be in question. Also an aleatory contract may be in question when the purchaser obliges himself to pay the purchase price for things that will arise in the future regardless of whether expectations will come true and regardless of their amount and quality (e.g., purchase of future harvested crop). A part of a main thing may not be the object of sale being not an independent thing under law.

(b) Price is a monetary consideration for the subject matter of sale contract. It must be expressed in money, otherwise there is no sale contract. The amount of sale price is given by agreement while respecting generally binding price regulations (if they exist) under the sanction of relative invalidity.[20] Maturity of obligation to pay sale price may be agreed as desired. Usually one of the following ways is used:

   - payment upon the delivery and receiving the subject matter of sale (typically for sale in shop);
   - following the delivery and receiving the object of sale contract (e.g., based on invoice) or possibly following ownership title transfer (after registration in the Land Registry);
   - prior to delivery and receiving the object of sale contract.

If the moment of maturity of obligation to pay sale price has not been agreed upon, the purchaser is generally obliged to pay the price on the first day after he was required

20. In a non-entrepreneurial one-off sale of a thing, the seller does not misuse his economic position even if he has an excessive economic profit from the agreed sale price; such a profit does not invalidate the contract of sale (ruling 2 Cdo 2/1998).

to pay by the seller. Also the way of payment (in cash, by credit transfer) and non-recurring or instalment payment is governed by agreement.[21]

Sale contract arises as soon as the parties have agreed upon its content. For a contract to be valid, written form is required only if the object of sale is a real property, otherwise it may be concluded as desired.

The so-called accessory/collateral agreement may make a part of the sales contract. The Civil Code contains more detailed provisions for three of them:

- Retention of title, by which a general principle of transferring ownership title to property by taking the thing over is modified. It may be agreed upon sale of movables only and the agreement must be concluded in writing. Its effect is that the purchaser obtains ownership right only upon full sale price payment.
- Pre-emption right, establishing a duty for the thing's owner, in case of his wish to alienate the thing (in the way as stated in the contract, or under law – by sale only), to offer an option to the former owner (the seller) to purchase it. Pre-emption right is of obligatory nature under law even though effects in rem may be agreed upon, but on the side of the purchaser only (pre-emption right does not pass on to heirs as a title and may not be transferred to another person). The agreement with effects in rem must be concluded in writing. Registration in the Land Registry is necessary for a pre-emption right with effects in rem to arise and therefore it can be concluded only in relation to real property registered in the Land Registry. If pre-emption right has been violated, the contract is not invalid, but the party entitled may claim to be offered the purchase of the thing by the assignee, or his pre-emption right will be preserved, that is, this assignee must offer him the thing if he wants to alienate it.
- Repurchase right entitles the seller to demand from the purchaser to sell him back the sold thing after a certain time. The length of the time may be agreed upon, otherwise repurchase right may be claimed only no later than one year after the delivery of the thing to the purchaser. In repurchase reserve, the person entitled may option in the term stated to decide to obtain back the thing sold. An alienation contract by which the repurchase right was violated is void.

Except for explicitly provided accessory clauses, other collateral agreements may be concluded, for example, a repurchase reserve entitling the purchaser to sell back the item bought back to the seller within a certain time, as well as a number of other reserves and terms admitting the termination of legal relation arising from a sales contract (a better purchaser reserve, etc.).

Sale contract is provided under §§588–600 Civil Code. If the object of sale between businesses is a movable thing – goods, the whole provision of commerce contracts, not only provision of contact of sales contract, contained in the Commercial Code (§§261–475) will be applied.

Rights and obligations of the parties to the contract in sale contract are both mutual and mutually conditioned as sale contract – this is a typical example of synallagmatic contracts.

21. Right to have the sale price reimbursed because of the sale contract not being made is a right resulting from unjust enrichment (R 27/2002).

Namely, the following rights and obligations originate from a sales contract for the parties to the contract:

- The seller's duty to perform properly the object of sale, that is, the duty to deliver the object of sale at the time as agreed by the parties. The moment of delivery is important for acquiring title to a movable thing. Along with ownership right, acquiring a risk of accidental perishing and accidental deterioration of the sales object is passed on the purchaser, unless agreed otherwise. If the purchaser acquired the ownership title even before, the seller owes the rights and duties of a bailee by the time the thing has been delivered (see explanation of bailment).
- The seller is bound to perform without unreasonable delays, but time of performance may be agreed on, too, or another term may be usual (see order sale). The seller is entitled to refuse to deliver the object of sale if the purchaser has not paid the price on time (unless agreed otherwise). If the object of sale is posted to the place of performance or place of destination, the purchaser is not bound to pay the price before he has the chance to look at the object of sale (necessary namely in cash-on-delivery sale). The seller also bears the costs related to the sales object delivery (unless agreed otherwise), namely, the measuring, weighing, and packaging costs.

The purchaser is bound to take over the subject of sale tendered properly and on time. If he is in delay with the takeover, the seller may deposit the sale object in a public storage facility or in other bailment at the cost of the purchaser, or he may sell the object, after notifying the purchaser, at the cost of the purchaser. In case of perishable goods and lack of time, notification is not necessary.

It is a duty of the seller to notify the purchaser about the defects of the thing, if he is aware of them. This duty should be fulfilled at the moment of conclusion of the contract of sale. If a defect appears later which the purchaser was not notified about by the seller (who may not have known about it) and which existed at the time of delivery, the purchaser is entitled to:

- remain a contractor and demand a discount from the agreed sale price, the amount of reduction corresponding with the nature and extent of the defect. The purchaser has this right regardless of the type of defect (both removable and non-removable);
- to rescind contract if the defect makes the thing unserviceable.

The defect that became apparent later is a defect that the thing had at the time of delivery; it is not a defect that was notified about by the seller. If the seller assured the purchaser that the thing had certain properties, namely, those demanded by the purchaser, or that the thing had no defects, and this assurance proves to be untrue, the purchaser may rescind the contract even if the defect does not make the thing unserviceable.

The defects must be reported by the purchaser without an unreasonable delay. Liability for defective products may be claimed in court only if the purchaser submitted an objection to the seller within twenty-four months since taking possession of the thing, if these are not things that go bad quickly or are used. The purchaser can demand recovery of costs incurred due to defective performance. The purchaser may claim the recovery in court only if having notified the seller about them in the same terms stated for claiming defects. If the purchaser has claimed the right arising from liability for defects, his right to recovery of damages is not affected.

The legal relation arising from contract of sale is terminated by the usual ways of contract discharge, mainly by performance. In addition to this, a frequent reason for a contract discharge is withdrawal; consequences of a collateral agreement (e.g., resolutive conditions) may be employed, too.

I. Exchange (Barter) Contract

103. Exchange is a legal relationship arising from an exchange contract and by which the parties have both right and obligation to exchange mutually a thing for a thing. Purchase contract provisions will be applied as appropriate in such a manner that each party is considered as the supplier and the purchaser at the same time. Appropriate application of the sales contract provisions means that the provisions consistent with the character of the exchange contract will be used (e.g., the provision on purchase price will not be applied).

Exchange contract related to business activities is governed by the Commercial Code.

II. Sale of Goods in Shops

104. The provisions on sale of goods in shops regulating situations when a business (natural or artificial legal person) sells goods within its business activities concentrate predominantly on the purchaser's protection and involve some kinds of sale and its consequences, quality and quantity rules and remedies for a non-conforming performance.

Among the particular types of sales, sale on order is explicitly regulated when such things are sold, the nature of which requires so as well as items sold only exceptionally by the business. The businessman is obliged to procure the thing ordered within a term agreed, if it is not agreed on, then within a reasonable time, otherwise the ordering party is entitled to withdraw from the contract. By withdrawal, his right to recovery of damages is not affected.

Provisions concerning the consequences of taking over the thing a specification of the moment of acquiring ownership of the thing purchased, namely, in case of mail-order sale and self-service sale, are worth attention. Two exceptions to the general rule that the title is acquired upon taking possession of the thing by the purchaser are:

- mail-order sale when the purchaser acquires the title upon taking possession of the thing but at the place of delivery determined by him;
- self-service sale when the transfer of the title to the thing purchased occurs at the moment of paying the price for the chosen goods. By this moment, the purchaser may return the chosen goods to their original place (if the purchaser damages or destroys the chosen goods before acquiring the title, he is liable for damage under general provisions on liability for damage).

Performances that are not usually linked to the sale of a thing must be agreed on. These are situations when the purchaser demands special packaging (gift package, delivery of goods to his residence, etc.).

Liability for damage can be distinguished as:

(a) Liability for defects arising from the seller's liability for the defects which the sold thing has after being taken by the purchaser. This liability does not relate to the things used if the defects are caused by their use or wear, or the things sold at lower prices if the price reduction was provided due to the defect in question.
(b) Warranty liability – liability for defects arising after taking possession of the thing by the purchaser. Under warranty liability, a warranty under law (the terms stipulated directly by law) and contractual warranty (arising from a contract or by accepting a one-sided declaration made in the certificate of guarantee the content of which may not be narrower to that stated under law) can be distinguished. Warranty under law applies to sale of goods that are not perishable or used. General warranty period is twenty-four months. In the Slovak legal regulation, there is a lack of a special regulation of liability for defects that have arisen due to a non-professional assembly or another non-professional way of putting something into operation.

§2. 'Commercial' Sale

105. Under the Commercial Code, the sale contract is established by the seller's obligation to deliver a movable asset (goods) determined separately as to the quantity and kind and transfer the respective property rights on the purchaser, and the purchaser's obligation to pay the selling price.

Fundamental elements of the contract are:

(1) the parties denoted;
(2) subject matter of sale sufficiently expressed;
(3) sale price as agreed.

The price must be agreed in the contract, or at least the manner of its subsequent determination must be outlined therein. Contract of sale may be concluded even without stating the selling price, presuming that the will of the parties to contract arises from the negotiation about making the contract. A contract of sale not containing an agreement on the selling price or an express agreement that the contract is concluded without expressly stating the selling price is deemed not concluded under law.

Sale contract involving relationships between businesses is comprehensively regulated under the Commercial Code. Even though a comprehensive provision for sale contract is included in the Civil Code as well, not a single provision for contract of sale under the Civil Code applies to the relationships between businesses.

Under the Commercial Code, contract of sale can be concluded orally, too.

Subject matter of sale contract can be movable assets only. In case of immovable things, basically the provisions under the Civil Code apply. The exceptions allowing application of the Commercial Code are as follows:

- contract of sale of an enterprise involving immovable things as parts of the enterprise;
- contract of sale of a thing leased, where the subject matter of the lease and the following sale may be a real property, too.

The seller is obliged under the contract to deliver the goods to the purchaser as determined under the contract, individually or in kinds, and to transfer ownership title to the goods on the purchaser. Title transfer is not carried out through a special act of the seller. Under the law, the seller should enable the purchaser to obtain title to the goods according to the contract and the law. It means for the seller to behave in such a manner as he obliged under the contract. If the contract does not contain such an agreement, the law itself supposes transfer of the title from the seller to the purchaser.

As for the manner of the sale price bargaining, there are several options available. The simplest way to bargain on the price is to agree on a specified amount of a particular valid currency. This amount may be defined directly in the contract, or reference to a price list may be included in the contract, which makes it part of the contract. The price is thus defined either by a total amount for the quantity of goods as agreed, or it is a price for a unit of goods and the total amount arises by multiplying the number of units by the unit price. It is also possible not to determine the price in the contract but a specific procedure may be agreed by the seller and the purchaser, allowing the price to be determined after conclusion of the contract. Such procedure is a specific way of determining the price. Parties to the contract may also agree that the price will be determined by a third party. If the seller and the purchaser explicitly agree that the price is not an essential part of the contract an optional provision of the Commercial Code is applied. In a case, the seller may demand the price to be paid that was usual for such or similar goods at the time of conclusion of the contract, under the terms similar to those included in the contract. However, this optional provision may be onerous for the seller due to the price growth of the same or similar goods occurring after conclusion of the contract. In order to take into consideration economic influences on the price growth the contractual parties may agree on a price clause to be included in the contract.

The law does not impose performance to be the essential element of a contract. If a stipulation on time of delivery is not included in the contract, the seller is bound, without the purchaser's call, to deliver the goods at an appropriate time with regard to the nature of the goods and place of delivery.

The goods that are subject matter of a sale contracts need not always be goods prepared for delivery, they may be goods to be produced. The essential feature of the contract of work is the fact that the subject of performance does not yet exist and the producer is supposed to make it. The dividing line stated between the two contract types is set by law, which states as a criterion to distinguish sales contract and contracts for work the amount of items to be used for the goods production. If the goods to be produced will be made in a substantial part from the things provided by the contractual party to which the goods will be delivered, it is a contract for work. If the deliverer produces the goods from its own raw materials or procures the raw materials for its business activities, it is a contract of sale. Substantial part of the things intended for the goods production is not determined only as a majority. Decisive means whether for a certain type of goods the items used are decisive in the view of function and other features. Another dividing component between the sale contract and contract for work is whether the work itself prevails, that is, the personal efforts provided by the delivering contractual party prevails over the matter itself that is to be delivered. If such personal efforts prevail, it is always a contract for work. As stated in the part of the contract involving the contract for work, such work may only consist in an assembly of a thing.

The last criterion is the nature of the subject matter of performance. In the case of the contract for work, it is stipulated unambiguously that work always means making, assembling, maintaining, repairing, or adjusting a construction or its part. If this were not so, the aim of the contract would be obtaining a title to a real property not yet made. Therefore, special legal provisions in case of contract for work are necessary, stipulating unequivocally that in the case of building construction it is always contract for work.

As arising from the basic provisions, the main obligation of the seller is to hand over to the purchaser the subject matter of the contract, that is, a movable asset, called goods. Along with the movable asset (the goods), the seller is bound by law also to deliver the documents related to the goods production. Basically, these are documents of two kinds. First, these are documents necessary for taking over the goods, like bill of delivery, packaging bill, carriage note, and other accompanying documents. Another group includes the documents necessary for use of the goods, like test and other certificates, instruction for use; and other documents serving the buyer as an aid for proper handling of the goods, and also as a certificate that the goods has the properties required.

The seller is bound to deliver the goods to the purchaser in the particular manner, at the particular place and time. As in determining these essentials of goods delivery, decisive means contractual stipulations, the provision under law is of optional nature only. The basic manners of goods delivery are defined as follows:

- delivery of goods to the first carrier in favour of the purchaser, if the seller delivers the goods to the purchaser via carrier;
- takeover of the goods by the purchaser from the seller;
- a possibility for the seller to handle goods in the place selected.

Goods as the subject matter of the sales contract have certain properties. Physically it is determination of goods by their quantity, quality, and form (e.g., material, colour, etc.). Further, goods are packaged or provided in a certain manner for the purpose of transportation. Quality is one of the most important properties of goods. No contradiction between the quality agreed in the contract and the quality given by law may occur. No agreement on the quality, contrary to the Consumer Protection Act (Act No. 250/2007 Col., as amended) and Technical Requirements on Products Act (No. 264/1999 Col., as amended) may be made. It is established that it is mainly the duty of the producer, the carrier, and the distributor to bring safe products to the market. If a contract does not stipulate quality or form and these properties are not given by law, the optional provision of the Commercial Code stipulates that the seller is bound to deliver the goods of a quality and form suitable for the purpose stated under the contract. If the purpose has not been univocally stated by the contract, the goods, their quality, and make are to be suitable for the purpose as a rule intended for this type of goods. The goods should have usual properties, that is, the properties that a particular kind of goods comparable with another, same or similar, kind of goods has in the territory of the Slovak Republic.

106. As for liability for defects, the Commercial Code distinguishes between the seller's liability for the defects, and liability for the assumed guarantee. The goods agreed on may have material or legal defects, or both. Material defects mean that the goods do not have properties as stated by the contract, or at least those stipulated by the Commercial Code. Material defects include quality defects and quantity defects. In case of quantity defects, we must distinguish between delivering the goods in a quantity smaller than that stated in the accompanying documents and a partial performance. A partial performance means that the delivered quantity, although consistent with the quantity stated in the delivery documents, is smaller than that the deliverer was bound to deliver under the contract. If performance in parts was agreed under the contract and the seller acts according to the contract, he performs the contract as proper. If performance in parts was not agreed upon between the seller and the purchaser and the seller delivers less than he was supposed to under the contract, it is a breach of contract. This applies, presuming the quantity stated is the same as the quantity declared in the accompanying documents, but smaller than that given in the contract. A situation that goods are delivered, but different from what the seller was bound to under the contract, is resolved by law. Such performance is called *aliud* (performance of something else, but similar). However, it must be distinguished between *aliud*, that is, different, but similar goods than those stipulated by contract, and delivery of entirely different goods. Under law, *aliud* is not a breach of contract or a failure to deliver goods, it is deemed a fault.

As for an error in law, under law goods are legally defective if a third party's right is attached to them. This means predominantly industrial rights of a third party. If such a restriction was taken into account in the contract and the purchaser consented to it, these are properly delivered goods that are defective. If the seller has concealed a third party's right from the purchaser, it is a defective performance. As for the third party's right that is attached to the goods, if it is an industrial or intellectual property right, it is deemed defective under law if:

- the right stated enjoys legal protection under the law of the state in the territory of which the purchaser resides or carries out business;
- the seller, at the time of conclusion of the contract, was aware or bound to be aware when this right enjoys legal protection under law of the state in the territory of which the purchaser resides or carries out business, or according to the law of the state, where the goods were further to be sold or used and the seller was aware of this sale or place of use at the time of conclusion of the contract.

Under the Commercial Code, a claim from legal errors does not accrue to the purchaser, if the purchaser was aware of the third party's right at the time of conclusion of the contract, or the seller was bound by the contract in performing his duties to proceed according to the instructions submitted to him by the purchaser.

In case of material defects, it should be noted that even in case of purchase contract the seller may use the items delivered by the purchaser for making the respective goods. Thus, it may happen that the material defects may originate in the items passed on by the purchaser for the goods production. In such a case under the Commercial Code, the seller principally is not liable for the defects. However, the seller has to prove that he exercised all reasonable care and could not discover the unsuitability of these items for the goods production, or he may have noted about them the purchaser, who, however, insisted on their use. If the seller has discovered defects of the items given to him by the purchaser, he should notify the purchaser. If the purchaser still insists on their use, the seller is not liable for the defective goods.

An essential precondition for a successful remedy of defects of the goods is reporting the defects to the purchaser. The Commercial Code does not apply a commonly used remedy, the complaint, but it uses the wording 'to report defects'. Under the Commercial Code, the buyer is bound to report to the seller the defects without a delay, after he has inspected the goods, or was supposed to do so. The purchaser is bound to report to the seller the apparent defects immediately after he has discovered them. The purchaser is bound to report to the seller the concealed defects of goods immediately after he has discovered them, either himself, or with the help of an expert. There is a statutory bar for reporting defects, which is two years after the goods have been delivered. The time limitation stated for reporting defects is a statutory bar, but unlike other general statutory bars under the Commercial Code, this one can be shortened or prolonged by agreement. If the purchase has not complied with the time limitation stated after claiming statutory warranty, it does not result in termination of his right to claim liability for damage. His position, however, will be worse in a possible court action as the purchaser may claim statutory bar and the complaint will be dismissed on these grounds. The effects of laches at the time stated by law do not apply to the purchaser under the Commercial Code, if the defective goods result from the facts the seller was aware of or must have been aware of at the time of the goods delivery.

As for the claims from defective performance of the seller, the law distinguishes whether the contract was breached in a substantial way or in a non-substantial way. The definition of substantial breach of contractual duty can be found in the Commercial Code and the sale contract has no respective special provisions. If a contract is breached in a substantial way by delivering of faulty goods, the purchaser is entitled to:

(1) removing the defects free of charge by delivering substitute goods instead of the faulty ones, by delivering the missing goods (in quantity faults) and removing errors in law;
(2) removing the defects by repair, presuming that defects can be repaired; or
(3) by an appropriate selling price reduction; or
(4) withdrawal from the contract.

Thus, the purchaser has the choice, but in case of defects that cannot be removed, logically he cannot demand removing the defects free of charge. The purchaser should necessarily report his choice with at the time limit stated under the Commercial Code, or immediately after reporting the defects. If the purchaser makes his choice during the time of limitation set by law, his rights in liability for damage will be restricted only to the rights given to him by law in case of non-substantial breach of contract. The purchaser who has chosen a certain claim in liability for faulty products cannot change this choice by a one-sided act. However, there are exceptions to this principle as follows:

- Under the Commercial Code when the purchaser deems certain defects to be reparable and demands removing the defects free of charge and the fault will prove irreparable or the repair would affect inappropriately the seller by incurring unreasonable costs to him, the purchaser may unilaterally change this choice to the next claim from those previously listed, that is, delivery of a substitution of the goods.
- The second exception is the case when the seller is delayed in obligation to remove the defects in an appropriate delivery period. In such case, the purchaser may, instead of the originally made choice for defects removal, demand either a reasonable price reduction or he may withdraw from the contract. Withdrawal is, however, possible on the part of the purchaser only when the goods may be returned in the same state in which he has received them.

Under the Commercial Code, the purchaser has, in addition to the right to claim liability for faulty products, also right to recovery for damage, arising as the result of defective performance as well as right to liquidated damages. It must be emphasized that only such damage is taken into consideration that is not settled by satisfying the right in liability for defects. It means that certain defects have been removed but another property loss accrued to the purchaser as a result. An essential limit for a possible recovery for damage is the provision of the Commercial Code, under which satisfaction attainable by claiming some of the rights in faulty goods liability cannot be obtained by claiming on another legal ground. The purchaser therefore cannot select recovery for damage simultaneously with claiming liability for faulty goods, neither can he claim satisfying his right through claiming unjustified enrichment. The Commercial Code mentions damage in relation to sale contract also in connection with a withdrawal from contract and instances of so-called facultative compensation and other claims related to a contract termination resulting from rescission by either party.

Under the Commercial Code, in case of non-substantial breach of contract the purchaser has more restricted rights as compared to those in case of substantial breach of contract. It means that under law the purchaser may only demand a removal of defects, or substitution of the missing amount of goods, or a sale price reduction. In case of non-substantial breach of contract, the purchaser basically cannot withdraw from the choice once made and cannot change it. Choice of claims towards the seller must be made as soon as possible after discovering defects by the purchaser. If he fails to do so, the seller is bound to remove the defects in a way stated by law, according to his own choice.

If the seller has not removed defects in goods within the time limitation appropriate to the nature of contract and provided subsequently by the purchaser, the purchaser is entitled to claim a sale price reduction, or to rescind the contract. The intent to rescind the contract must be communicated to the seller, though. In case of reduction, the purchaser may reduce the price from the price as stated in the seller's invoice or may demand it from the seller after paying the price. The purchaser is not bound to pay the part of the sale price corresponding with his claim to reduction until the seller has removed the defects. This provision does not apply if the impossibility to return the goods in the state thereby stated is not caused by acts or omissions of the purchaser, or if a change of the goods condition occurred as a result of inspection properly carried out in order to ascertain defects of goods. Finally, the purchaser may rescind the contract if, before discovering defects, he has sold the goods, their part, or partly consumed or changed them in the course of their usual use. In this case, the purchaser is bound to return back unsold, unused, or changed goods and to provide compensation to the seller in the amount he enriched himself.

107. As for obtaining title to the goods, the purchaser obtains it under the Commercial Code at the instant he has obtained title to dispose of the goods (delivery). The contract may, however, stipulate that the purchaser obtains ownership title in another moment, too. First, it is possible to agree under the contract that the purchaser will obtain ownership title prior to the goods delivery. Such agreement must be concluded in a written form as prescribed by law. Another condition is that such goods are sufficiently objectively defined. Problem is not with goods stated individually, but with goods denoted in kind, which must be specially labelled or separated from other goods. Under the Commercial Code, an agreement may be stipulated under the contract that the purchaser will obtain title to the goods only after their delivery. Again, such agreement must be made in writing. Unless agreed otherwise, the purchaser will not obtain title to the goods, if the payment was partial, but only after paying fully for the goods.

The principle that no one may transfer more rights upon another than he himself has, does not apply in sale contracts concluded under the Commercial Code. For this reason under the Commercial Code, the purchaser obtains title to the goods also if the seller was not the owner of the goods. However, the purchaser will not become an owner of the goods, if he was aware of, or could be aware of the fact that the seller was not the goods owner and is not authorized to dispose of it.

If, according to the contract, the seller has returned the goods to the purchaser, the purchaser is bound to take possession of the goods and to pay the seller the price agreed. The sale price may be paid in cash or in another way. It may be stipulated under the contract that the sale price will be paid upon the delivery of goods or the respective documents, or by a cheque or by a bill of exchange, or by a letter of credit. The purchaser is bound by law to pay the sale price, when the seller, according to the contract and law, enables the purchaser to dispose of the goods or the documents enabling the purchaser disposal of the goods. A typical document is the bill of lading which functions as a security. If the seller is bound by the contract to dispatch the goods, he may do so, under the condition that the purchaser will be given the goods or respective documents upon paying the sale price. However, the seller is not entitled to act in this way if it is inconsistent with the respective contractual terms. The purchaser is not bound to pay the sale price if he has no opportunity to inspect the goods.

The law mentions instances where a party breaches the contractual duties and bears risk of damage. The other party, which has such goods on his premises, is bound to take reasonable care to prevent the goods from damage or destruction. If a contract party neglects such a duty, the party is liable for damage to the extent, to which it was able to prevent it by its acting. Further, the Commercial Code provides for a deadline where the purchaser is in delay with taking over the goods or paying the selling price if the goods delivery and sale price payment are supposed to occur simultaneously. In such situation the seller, who has the goods on his premises, or he has not, but is entitled to dispose of them, must take reasonable measures to preserve the goods. Under law, the seller is entitled to retain the goods until the purchaser has paid to him reasonable costs accrued as a result of withholding the goods. The Commercial Code regulates the situation when the purchaser has taken possession of the goods but intends to refuse them. The goods thus are available to the purchaser and he is bound by law to take reasonable measures to preserve the goods. The purchaser is bound to retain the goods by the time the seller has paid to him appropriate costs accrued as a result of storing the goods.

A manner of delivery by a carrier is stipulated. Under this provision when, after the goods being delivered to their destination the purchaser has an opportunity to dispose of the goods and he wants to reject the goods, he is bound to take over the goods and keep it on his premises at the cost of the seller. This duty is not imposed by law on the purchaser if the seller, or a person authorized by him to take care of the goods, is present in the place of performance. The duty to store the goods can be satisfied by placing them in a third party's storage at the cost of the other party to the contract. Between the party to the contract and the third party, a contract of storage relationship arises.

In business contract relationships, a contract of exchange, related to business activities of parties, is governed by provisions of the Commercial Code on sale contract. This makes the contract of exchange different from other contracts concluded between businesspersons in relation to their business activities that are not provided by the Commercial Code but are stipulated under the Civil Code. In business contract relationships either party to the contract of exchange has the position of a seller.

I. Sale (Transfer) of the Enterprise

108. Under an enterprise sale contract, the seller obliges himself to hand over to the purchaser an enterprise and to transfer title to the enterprise, and the purchaser obliges himself to take over the obligations of the seller related to the enterprise and pay the sale price. The contract must be concluded in writing and needs the attested signature of the parties. Enterprise sale contract establishes an absolute sale and it is entirely regulated by the Commercial Code, while the Civil Code contains no such or similar contract relationship. The Commercial Code stipulations on enterprise sale are mostly non-mandatory.

The subject matter of sale is an enterprise and the law does not require the particular items, rights, or other values to be specified under the contract; however, the enterprise itself, or its part that is subject to the sale, must be individualized. An essential of the contract is the enterprise denoted, or its part, being subject to the sale, the obligation of the seller to hand over the enterprise to the purchaser and to transfer on him the title to the enterprise, and the purchaser's obligation to take over the seller's obligations related to the enterprise and to pay the selling price. As for determining the selling price it must be taken into account that a subject matter of sale as a rule is an enterprise that is under operation and whose business assets constantly vary, while as a rule some time has run between conclusion of the contract and the instant when it has become effective. Basically, selling price is deemed to be stated by giving the sum of things, rights, and obligations stated in the books of accounts of the enterprise sold upon the day of conclusion of the contract and based on other values stated in the contract, unless they are included in the accountancy. If the contract is to become effective on a later date, the purchase price sum will be changed in relation to the increase or reduction of assets accruing in the meantime. If the enterprise transferred includes a real property, the will manifestations of the parties must be expressed in the same document. Under law, all rights and obligations related to the sale are passed on to the purchaser. However, only property rights (including ownership) are passed over, not other rights (e.g., trading certificate). The purchaser, who obtained the enterprise upon contract, may continue to carry out business under the current company name and succession clause, unless it was contrary to the law or a right of a third person. Transfer of a business company without a transfer of an enterprise, that is, without enterprise sale contract, is basically inadmissible. However, transfer of company is possible when transferring only a part of the enterprise, if the business of the rest of the enterprise will be carried out under another company name or if this part of enterprise has been wound up.

Transfer of debts is governed by rules of assignment of claim under the Civil Code. For the assignment to be effective a notice of assignment served on the debtor, or a proof of assignment by the seller, is required. Before this notice or proof, the debtor may perform his obligation to his original creditor, that is, the seller. Unlike general stipulation under the Civil Code in relation to debt take over requiring the creditor's consent, under a special provision of the Commercial Code in enterprise sale such consent is not necessary to transfer an obligation, but the seller is directly bound by law to guarantee for performing the transferred obligations by the person who has bought the obligation. In relation to transfer of debts and obligations, in the interests of legal certainty, the law imposes the seller to notice the debtors without delay on the respective transfer of debts on the purchaser, and to announce to the purchaser the obligations takeover to the respective creditors.

In order to protect the original owner's creditors, the creditors of the current enterprise owner to raise an objection in court (actionability) within sixty days following the day when they were informed about the enterprise sale but no later than six months after the sale has been entered in the Trade Register, may ask the Court to rule that the obligation transfer by the seller upon the purchaser is most ineffective for them. If the seller is not recorded in the Trade Register, the objection in court may be raised within sixty days following the day the creditor has learned about the enterprise sale, but no later than six months following conclusion of the contract. The ground for the complaint must be a doubtless impairment of the debt recoverability compared to the condition of the given enterprise prior to its sale. If the creditor succeeds in his complaint, the seller is bound to perform the obligation towards him when matured and is entitled to demand the performance as provided along with the ancillary rights.

All the rights, arising from industrial or other intellectual property involving business activities of the enterprise on sale are transferred by law on the purchaser, too. The transfer does not involve the rights of personal nature which, according to the law, are non-transferrable.

Based on the mandatory provisions, the rights and obligations arising from ownership of enterprise towards the enterprise employees are passed from the seller on the purchaser. Rights and obligations of employees are specified closely under the Labour Code and employment contract.

Upon the day of the enterprise sale contract becoming effective, which as a rule – unless stipulated otherwise by the contract – is identical with the time of conclusion of the contract, the seller is bound to transfer, and the purchaser to take over the items included in the sale contract. The record of sale is required to be made in writing and signed by both parties. The content of this record involving the passing over and the taking over are both movable assets as well as the real property that are subject matter of the contract. By the takeover, the risk of damage is passed over from the seller on to the purchaser. Regarding usually extensive property in enterprise sale, the risk is passed over gradually in the process of passing over and taking over. Non-mandatory stipulation of the Commercial Code, however, enables to stipulate the transfer of subject matter in a different way. Title to all movable assets is obtained under law upon the day as stipulated by the contract to be effective, and all other rights and property values as well as obligations are transferred, too. On the contrary, title to the respective real property is obtained only upon the entry in the Land Registry. If the entry to the Land Registry were denied, the seller has the duty to remove all obstacles, because the contract has become effective upon signing the record of taking over. Failure to perform this duty by the seller can be resolved under liability of the seller for errors in law concerning the sold enterprise.

Reference of the Commercial Code to similar stipulations involves only movable things, as the stipulations concern movable assets only, while real property cannot be subject to sale under the Commercial Code. Ownership title to movables therefore may be passed on the earlier or later day, if so agreed by the parties to the contract, that is, at a time different from that of the contract becoming effective. Under the Commercial Code the purchaser may, under an enterprise sale contract, obtain title to movables from the non-owner, too.

The Commercial Code provisions contain a special liability provision for defects of the enterprise on sale. Missing items, faulty items, and errors in law are distinguished.

The provisions related to enterprise sale as a whole apply also for the contracts under which a part of an enterprise, which is a separate organization unit, is sold.

If the seller is a person registered in the Trade Registry, the cogent stipulation of the Commercial Code demands this sale be entered in the Trade Registry. In such a case, the seller will propose the filing of the respective entry. The collection of documents, making part of the Trade Registry, contains also a contract for sale of the enterprise or its part.

II. Sale of a Leased Thing

109. The Commercial Code in its basic provision stipulates that upon the contract for sale of a thing leased the parties agree in the lease contract (a lease contract concluded under the Civil Code or in the contract on the lease of a means of transport under the Commercial Code (*see* more below), or after its conclusion that the lessor is entitled to buy the thing hired, or a set of the things hired with at the time of the lease contract being effective, or after its termination. This contract must be concluded in writing and involves the so-called relative business.

Fundamental contract terms are:

- the parties to the contract denoted: the lessor and the lessee;
- an agreement on the lessee's right to buy the thing leased;
- denoting the thing involved;
- denoting the time for the lessee to exercise this right.

If the lessee is by contract entitled to buy the thing leased, the contract will terminate upon delivery of a written notice on performing this right according to the contract of the operational lease, even though it was a fixed-term contract (therefore both fixed-term contracts and contracts for indefinite duration are thus terminated). If the lessee is entitled by the contract of the operational lease to buy the thing only after lapse of the contract term, this right becomes extinct, if the party entitled has not notified the other party in writing without delay its will to buy the thing hired after termination of the lease contract. Upon contract of sale, the title to the movable asset is passed over to the purchaser. The title to a real estate is passed over upon entry in the Land Registry. Risk of damage is passed over to the purchaser upon the conclusion of contract of sale.

Unless the sale price decisive in exercising the right to buy the hired thing is determined, or the manner of its determination, the purchaser is bound to pay the sale price at which such or comparable goods are usually sold at the time of conclusion of the contract. The purchaser is bound to pay the sale price without delay after the contract of sale becomes effective.

When assessing the defects, decisive is the properties presumed for the leased thing. The term for reporting the defects of the thing bought begins to run following the day when the lessee has taken over the thing leased. If the title to the thing leased has not passed to the purchaser and the seller has not removed the defects within a reasonable time stated by the purchaser, the purchaser may rescind the contract.

The contract may stipulate that after certain time since the contract of lease has become effective the lessee is entitled to obtain title to the thing leased if he performs this right towards the lessor. In such a case, the person attaining the title to the thing leased is not entitled to claim defects of the leased thing, except for the legal defects being *errors in law*, unless he has a quality warranty provided.

The wording of the law makes apparent the leading concept of the Commercial Code arising from freedom to contract. It arises not only from the non-mandatory character of a major part of the text of the Commercial Code, but also from the fact that the respective law is only a framework for conclusion of contracts. Contract basically arises upon an agreement of the parties on its content as a whole, which may be rather extensive in the cases resolved.[22] If the contract concluded was not that of sale of the leased thing but a lease contract, it would be deemed an unnamed contract.

22. General conditions of leasing are binding for parties to the contract of lease with subsequent sale. This binding effect may only be ended by manners resulting from the contract or from the law. Therefore, if parties to the contract have agreed that the difference between payment of premium and the actual damage from the insured event is borne by the lessee, he cannot successfully claim in court reimbursement of the difference pursuant to the legal regulation (ruling 1 Cdo 94/1995).

Chapter 3. Donation

110. Donation as a legal relationship arises by deed, by which the donor gratuitously gives or promises to give gratuitously something to the donee, and the donee accepts the gift or the promise of gift. Donation is not a unilateral juridical act. There is no donation if the property benefit it assigned without the will to make a deed of donation. Deed of donation is subject to a uniform legal regulation in the Civil Code for both private and business legal relationships.

Elements of deed of donation are gratuitousness (lack of consideration) and free will. Gratuitousness means that the donee is not legally bound to provide consideration for the gift. There is no donation if the property benefit is assigned based on a legal obligation and not at free will (e.g., maintenance duty performing).

A donation deed generally does not require any specific form, unless the gift is given and taken at the moment of donating. The respective deed must be made in writing. Also donation of immovable things must be made in writing, which is dictated by the character of the donation (in order to acquire title to a real property registered in the Land Registry a registration in the Land Registry is necessary). The law explicitly stipulates that such donation deed is invalid that is to be performed only after the donor's death (*donatio mortis causa*). In this way, inheritance rights are protected. Some consequences of donation carried out during the donor's life may, however, have an effect after his death, by being included in the respective inheritance portion.

The most important obligation and right of a donor is to provide gratuitous property performance to the donee. The donee has a respective right and obligation to accept the gift. The donor is also bound to notify about defect of the gift if he knows about them, when offering the donation.

If the thing has a defect that the donor did not notify the donee about, the donee is entitled to return the thing but only if the defect had existed at the time of donation and it did not occur later. The right of the donee to return the gift is generally subject to the limitation period of three years. This period runs since the day when the defect could have been commonly observed by the donee.

Donation as a legal relationship terminates due to general causes of obligation discharge, most often by performance.

A specific cause of termination of donation (or legal effects of donation) allows cancelling the legal relationship in case when the donor demands the gift be returned as the donee behaves to him and his family in a way that is *contra bonos mores.*[23]

23. Donation is discharged on the basis of a unilateral legal act made by the donor against the donee who grossly breached good morals (R 88/1998).

Chapter 4. Contract for Work

§1. 'Civil' Contract for Work

111. Contractual relationship, the purpose of which is a work to be performed, arises from a contract for work. This is a contract, by which one party (provider) obliges himself to the other party (client) to provide work for this party at his own risk and for remuneration. The rise of the contract is bound to the agreement of contractual parties on fundamental essentials, such as determining the work, the remuneration and carrying out the work at the risk of the provider. The Civil Code prescribes no special form for this contract to be valid (however, general provisions state that a building – a real property – contract must be concluded in writing). Unless the work is performed while waiting, the provider is bound to provide the client with a written note of receiving the order. The Civil Code stipulates the following essentials of the written note: the object of work, its extent, quality, the term, and the remuneration for the work to be performed. If the provider does not give a written note, it is not a reason for the contract to be void.

The work is defined as a kind of work where the result is usually of a material character, based on producing, repairing, or adjusting, or possibly destroying a thing, but it may have a non-material character, too.

The remuneration – price – may be determined by a contract, by special regulations or pursuant to the Civil Code. If the price has not been agreed upon or stipulated by a regulation, the Civil Code stipulates a reasonable price to be provided.

A fundamental element of a contract is to carry out the work at one's own risk. It is up to the contractor how he will perform the work. He also bears the risk in case of such circumstances barring him from performing the contract as proper. The most frequent instances are:

- risk of the work frustration;
- risk of frustration of the work performed, but not yet delivered.

In all cases of contracts for work, the parties to the contract have the following rights and obligations:

- The provider is bound to perform the work according to the contract. This obligation comprises a number of partial elements, including the issues who is supposed to carry out the work, what material will be used, in what way, what manner and what time period.
- An essential duty of the client is to pay the remuneration to the provider. This remuneration must be provided in the place as agreed by the parties. Unless agreed otherwise, this place will be the ordering provider's residence. The remuneration for the work is payable as a rule after the work has been performed (a different agreement is possible). If the work is to be performed in parts, or if performing

the work is very costly, the provider is entitled to demand a down payment as appropriate at the time when the work is being carried out. The provider has the right to the down payment as agreed even if the work has not been performed, if he was willing to carry out the work but he was frustrated by circumstances on the part of the client (the provider is bound to include what he has saved by non-performing the whole work, what he has earned in some other way or what earnings he purposefully missed).

- The provider is bound to notify the client without delay about the drawbacks of the material delivered by him which prevents the provider to do the work. The provider is bound in the same way when the client demands the work to be done according to unsuitable instructions.
- Both parties to the contract have right to rescind the contract.

The provider may withdraw from the contract if cooperation of a client was inevitable to carry out the work, and the client was given a reasonable time for doing so and nevertheless the client did not provide such cooperation. The provider has right to rescind the contract if he notifies the client about his failure to keep the term. The client may rescind the contract if the work apparently will not be carried out on time, or will not be carried out properly, or the provider does not go on working even if given an additional time.

The client may also rescind the contract if no breach of a legal obligation occurred, that is, at any time before the work has been finished but he is bound to pay to the provider an amount appropriate for the work already done, unless the provider may otherwise utilize its result, and reimburse him the necessary cost incurred.

The death of the client does not itself terminate the contract; however, it might cause the termination of the legal relationship due to the nature of the agreement or the purpose of the work (e.g., in ordering one's own portrait).

The death of the provider results in termination of the legal relationship only if the performance of the work depends on special abilities of the provider. If the provider has already carried out some partial acts in the performance of the work, his heirs may claim only reimbursement of usable material prepared for the work and a part of the remuneration appropriate to the usable results of the work done. If the contracting party cannot make use of anything of the providers work after his death, the heirs are entitled only to demand the reimbursement of used materials.

Producing a Thing as Ordered

112. The Civil Code provides for producing a thing as ordered as one of common cases of contract for work. Such a contract provides a right for the client to have a thing manufactured by the provider as ordered and the obligation arises for him to pay to the provider for producing the thing. The aim is to produce a new product according to requirements of the party ordering.

The Civil Code concentrates on liability in producing a thing as ordered; otherwise general provisions for contract for work apply. The provider has liability for defects, similarly as for defects of the sold goods. The provider is liable for the defects occurring after taking over the thing within warranty period. Similarly, he is liable for the thing to have properties required by the client. The provider will be also liable for defects of the ordered product caused by defective material delivered by the client, or unsuitability of his instructions unless he has notified the client about the defective material or on unsuitability of his instructions. Warranty period is two years. For things intended to be used for a longer time, special regulations stipulate warranty longer than two years (a longer warranty may concern only a single part of the product). As to the building construction warranty period is three years (implementing regulation may provide a shorter warranty period for certain parts of the construction, but not less than eighteen months).

Repair and Adjustment of a Thing

113. Another common contract for work involves repair and adjustment of a thing. Legal relationship arises from the contract under which the client has right to have a thing repaired or adjusted by the provider as ordered. The customer is bound to pay the price for the repair or adjustment to the provider. Repair of a thing is an activity by which defects, damage, or wear effects of a thing are removed, and adjustment is an activity through which a surface or properties of a thing are changed.

The Civil Code specifies, namely, liability for repair or adjustment defects. The provider is liable for the defects in the repair or adjustment carried out after the thing has been taken over by the client. This is liability under law. In addition, the provider is also liable for the defects occurring within warranty period. The general warranty period for such things is three months unless provided or agreed on otherwise (e.g., warranty period in building construction is at least eighteen months). The provider is also liable for the defects caused by a defective condition of the thing or unsuitability of the client's instructions unless the provider has notified the client about defective condition of the thing or unsuitable instructions.

§2. 'Commercial' Contract for Work

114. Under the Commercial Code, a contract for work constitutes an obligation of the worker to carry out certain work and the obligation of the party ordering to pay the price for the performance of work. Fundamental terms of the contract are, in addition to denoting of the parties, determination of the subject matter of the work and determination of the price for the work. No written form is prescribed for this type of contract.

The subject matter of the work is always a result of a certain activity. Such work may be producing a thing, unless falling within the scope of contract of sale: assembling, maintaining a thing (i.e., preserving the thing in the state suitable for use), its repairing (removing defects), or carrying out adjustments as agreed (updating, expansion). In addition to the activities described, any other activity, the result of which may be materially grasped, but not falling within another contract type, can be deemed as work. The price for work must be agreed on directly in the contract, or at least the manner of its determination must be stipulated in the contract. The exceptions are cases where the will of the parties is apparent from bargaining to conclude a contract without stating the price. For such cases, optional stipulations are available in law, according to which the client is bound to pay the price that is ordinarily paid for a work comparable, at the time of conclusion of the contract and under similar business terms.

Under the law, the following cases are deemed work (and not a contract of sale):

(1) when a major part of the party's obligation rests in carrying out an activity (i.e., the value of the work performed is higher than total material costs); or
(2) when subject matter of the obligation given involves also assembling the thing made (i.e., regardless of the above-mentioned criteria).

Further, work always means making, assembling, maintaining, repairing, or adjusting a building construction or its part (i.e., regardless of that, e.g., the nature of the building construction in question requires as a rule higher material costs that are the costs related to the activity). This legal provision is reasoned, namely, by the nature of the building as an immovable thing, and usually also by a longer time for its carrying out.

The provisions of the Civil Code that also stipulate contract for work do not apply here and therefore it is a 'relative business' (*see* above). However, the parties may agree in a written contract that the particular contract for work will be governed by the Commercial Code.

The provider is bound to carry out the work on his costs and risk, without the time agreed, otherwise in a time reasonable for the nature of the work. This stipulation implies dependence of a claim for the price on the successful completion of the work. The things the client is supposed to deliver at his cost and at his risk to the provider must be delivered within the time stipulated under the contract or without unnecessary delay. Consequences of breach of this duty are dealt with in the Commercial Code. The ordering party bears the risk of damage to the things he has procured for carrying out the work and remains their owner until they have become part of the object of work. This applies even when the things are placed in the premises of the provider, who is liable as a storage keeper in relation to them. Unless provided otherwise under the contract, the provider is bound to procure the things necessary for the work, and bears risk of damage to these things.

The Commercial Code contains a very special stipulation of rise of ownership to a thing that is subject to the given work. This stipulation is different from a general stipulation of obtaining ownership title under the Civil Code. Under the Commercial Code if the provider makes the thing within the client, on the ground owned or procured by him, the owner of the thing ordered is the client from the very beginning. In other cases – when the thing is being made on the provider's premises or elsewhere – the provider is the owner of the thing made. It is apparent from these provisions that rise of ownership is governed by the place where it is made and for the rise of ownership (e.g., to a building constructed) it is not therefore decisive as to which of the parties has procured the material necessary to carry out the work. Moreover, the Commercial Code stipulates that ownership of a thing that is subject to maintenance, repair, or adjustment does not pass on to the provider and the client remains the owner. However, the law expressly stipulates that the parties to the given contract for work may agree otherwise on bearing risk of damage on the thing made. In a case when the risk of damage is on the provider, this risk is passed on the client simultaneously with the ownership transfer.

In relation to establishing ownership to the performed work, the law establishes, also as a non-mandatory rule, a settlement of the parties to the contract for work in case of termination of obligations arising from this contract (e.g., by withdrawal from the contract), also in relation to which of the parties are liable for the particular obligation extinction. The client is bound to pay the price to the provider as agreed in the contract or stated in the manner given in the contract. Possible down payments, their amount depends on the agreement of the parties. In bargaining a particular price, it is necessary, in addition to the respective provisions of the Commercial Code, to adhere to the Act No. 18/1996 Col. on prices. The bargained price will not be influenced by the fact that the price was agreed on the basis of the budget – a certain accounted amount of costs plus the profit – that became part of the contract, or was announced to the client before conclusion of the contract. A price stated like this, as a rule, also has a nature of so-called fixed price and thus it is binding, regardless of the fact that the terms in which the budget was calculated may have changed. Parties to the contract are entitled to change unilaterally the price so determined only if so stipulated by contract or by law. The Commercial Code has named two respective instances when a change of price contrary to the budget may be claimed successfully:

- if it arises from the contract that the budget is not guaranteed as complete;
- if it arises from the contract that this budget is not considered binding.

Under the terms closely explained by the Commercial Code, the provider can claim increase of price.

If, after conclusion of the contract the parties agree on limiting the work extent, or, on the contrary, on its increasing, they are bound to agree on reasonable reduction or increase of the price agreed.

The client is bound to pay the price for the work at the time agreed in the contract, that is, also either prior to the obligation performance, or by means of so-called client's credit with the term of payment deferred. Only if the payment term has not been so stipulated under the contract, an optional stipulation in law exists that the right to payment arises by carrying out the work, that is, by its proper completing and handing over to the party ordering. Payment terms should be agreed by the contract.

Non-mandatory provisions of the Code specify the manner of performing the work agreed under the contract. In respect of this:

- The client is entitled to check the work while performing and if shortcomings are discovered, to demand them be removed when carrying out the work; the provider's failure to do so doubtlessly will result in a fundamental breach of contract, and the client will be entitled to withdraw from the contract.
- The provider is bound to inform the client without unnecessary delay about unsuitability of the things taken over from the client or the instructions given to him by the client for the work realization, if the provider could have found out this unsuitability after exercising reasonable care; the law further outlines other

steps of the parties to be done in such a case that are binding, and further relevant consequences.

- The provider is bound to inform the client without an unnecessary delay and to propose him a change of work, if having found hidden obstacles, when performing the work, and these obstacles prevent him from carrying out the work in the manner agreed; further steps of the parties and the respective solutions are described under the Commercial Code.
- If the client is entitled under the contract to check the subject matter of work in a certain phase of its completing, the provider is bound to invite the client on time to carry out such a check.

The provider will perform his duty to perform the work by its proper completing and passing over to the client in the place agreed, or in the place stipulated as optional under the Commercial Code. The client is in turn obliged to take over the work as proper. If the work has not been performed as proper (i.e., the provider has not fulfilled his obligation to perform the work, if the work is faulty – termination of obligation by its performance), the client is not bound to take over the work.

Therefore, in this respect. the parties should always agree under what terms the client is bound to take over the subject matter of work (mainly if it is a building). Commonly, parties agree that the client is bound to take over the work, if it only has faults that do not bar the use of the subject matter of work nor make its use substantially difficult. The manner of passing over and takeover must thus be appropriately agreed on in the contract and if either party so requires, passing over the subject matter of work will be recorded in writing and signed by both parties. By passing over and taking over a thing, the client obtains title to the thing, and the risk of damage to the thing is passed over on the client, too, if borne by the provider by that time.

A common proof of the work performed properly (namely, within investment construction building) is the test carried out on the basis of the parties' agreement. If such agreement has existed, the work has been completed as proper only after these tests have been successfully taken.

If the work involves other activity than making, assembling, maintaining, repairing, or adjusting a thing (e.g., a design, geological survey, computer programs), the provider is bound to proceed in this activity within the framework given by the contract, exercising reasonable care in such a manner as to obtain a materially tangible result of activity as stated under the contract. The provider is bound to pass over such a result to the client. Specific nature of such work implies that the materially grasped result is utilizable in some cases not for the client itself, but for other persons, too. Such result may be given to other persons only if so allowed by the contract for work. If the subject matter of work is a result of a creative activity, protected by intellectual or industrial rights, the client is entitled to employ it only for the purposes stated under the contract. He can use it for other purposes only upon the consent of the provider. Under the Commercial Code, the provider is liable, in carrying out all kinds of work for breach of right evolving from industrial or other intellectual property protected in the territory of the Slovak Republic. When violating such rights in the territory of another state the provider is liable only if at the time of conclusion of the contract he knew that the subject matter of work will be utilized (e.g., exporting the subject matter of work) in the territory of this state. In order to avoid this liability for work, the provider is therefore bound to inspect whether rights of third parties are not violated in the territory of the state where the subject of work will be utilized. The extent, consequences and further liability terms are stipulated by special regulations.

The work is faulty if it is inconsistent with the result stipulated under the contract. The provider is liable for the faults the work had at the time when it was passed on. If the risk of damage to the thing is passed on to the client only later, for example, according to the agreement of the parties to the contract or due to the provider's delay, the provider is liable under law for the *faults the* work has at the moment of passing on the risk (risk of damage to the thing made under the contract for work). The provider is also liable for the faults of the work arising only after passing on the work (passing on the risk of damage) if these faults were caused by breach of his duties (e.g., the faults arisen as a result of faulty operation instructions).

As with the contract of sale, the Commercial Code – unlike the Civil Code – does not stipulate implied warranty (warranty imposed by law). To provide warranty it is necessary to include a warranty clause in the contract or the provider may take it over by a unilateral declaration. The provider is liable, in the extent of the express warranty for the faults of the work related to the express quality warranty; therefore, an express warranty need not relate to all properties of the subject matter of the work. Warranty period related to the work starts by passing on the work. The stipulations involving contract of sale apply as appropriate for quality guarantee, involving also interruption of the warranty period and warranty reservations. If the work involves producing a thing, the Code establishes a similar application of sale contract stipulations about quantity, quality, make, and package, and some other provisions concerning faulty goods.

Consequences of unsuitability of the thing or instructions provided by the client upon the provider's liability for the faults of the given work are stipulated under the Commercial Code, whereby the provider is obliged to judge expertly the things and instructions provided by the client and to notify him on unsuitability of materials or instructions.

In relation to claiming the rights arising from liability for faults, the client is bound first to inspect the subject matter of work or arrange its inspection as soon as possible after passing the subject matter of work on. The Court will not grant the right arising from the liability for faulty work if the client has not informed the provider about the faults as specified:

- apparent faults, without an unnecessary delay, after he has found them or was supposed to find, while exercising reasonable care in their inspection which he was bound to do;
- hidden faults, that is, those found out later – without an unnecessary delay after having found them out or being able to find them out while exercising reasonable care, but no later than within two years and, in case of building constructions no later than within five years following the passing over of the subject matter of work. For faults covered by warranty, the warranty period applies instead.

In case of claims timely and properly submitted for faults in work, except for some diversion stipulated under the Commercial Code, the respective stipulations stated for sale contract apply as appropriate. In order to satisfy rights arising from liability for faults a principal distinction is made between the instance, when the contract was breached substantially as a result of faulty performance and instances when faulty performance was only a non-substantial breach of the given contract for work.

Chapter 5. Loans

§1. Loan for Consumption

115. Legal relationship arises from a loan contract where one party (the creditor) transfers the things stated in kind to the other party (the debtor) and the debtor obliges himself to return the things of the same kind after lapse of a fixed period. Fundamental essentials of the contract are handing over a thing, stating the generic thing in kind (unlike in borrowing and lease), temporality of the relationship, and the duty to return the thing of the same kind. As a rule, the subject matter of loan is money as an instrument of payment.

Basically, loans are classified according to the distinction into monetary and non-monetary loans.

Creditor is obliged to hand over the subject of loan and the debtor is bound to return the things of the same kind in the same amount and quality as he borrowed, at the time stated. However, parties may agree that the debtor will be bound to return a larger amount of the things or of a better quality. The debtor is bound to pay interests only if they have been agreed on. The amount of interests is not specified by law. Opposite to interests for delay, the loan interest should be understood as a payment for use of the surety borrowed. If the interests were agreed on in an inappropriate amount, the agreement will be void due to inconsistence with good morals.

§2. Loan for Use

116. Loan for use, called 'borrowing' in the Slovak law, is a legal relationship arising by contract under which the lender leaves the thing to the borrower for a gratuitous temporal usage. Significant elements of this contract are handing over of the thing for use, gratuitousness, and temporality. The objects of borrowing are only the things stated individually, and these things must be returned to the lender without impairing its substance. Borrowing differs from loan by the object and by gratuitousness from lease.

The lender is bound to hand over the thing to the borrower. If special rules are to be observed in the use of the thing borrowed, namely, if the use is governed by instructions for use or is regulated by a technology standard, the lender is bound to notify the borrower about it unless the rules are generally known.

The borrower is entitled and bound to use the thing as proper according to the purpose agreed under the contract or for the purpose the thing usually serves. The borrower is bound to protect the thing from damage, loss, or destroying. The thing borrowed may be handed over for use to another person only if explicitly agreed. The duty of the borrower is also to return the thing borrowed either after extinction of the legal relationship or even before lapse of time agreed for the borrowing as soon as he no more needs it. This duty is the same when, according to law, the lender has demanded returning the thing even before lapse of the time stated.

The Civil Code establishes for the lender liability for damage arising from the fact that he did not duly inform the borrower about special rules for the use of the thing.

The termination of the legal relation arising from the borrowing contract arises for a number of reasons, both common for all types of contracts and specific.

Common termination arises as responding to the purpose of borrowing, that is, namely, lapse of the time agreed for the borrowing, and performance of the purpose of borrowing. Specific reasons include termination of legal relationship arising from the demand of the lender to return the thing before lapse of the time agreed because the borrower does not use the thing as proper or use it inconsistent with the purpose to which it serves. A reason for termination is also when the borrower let another person use the thing without the lender's consent.

Chapter 6. Lease Contracts

§1. General Provisions

117. Under lease contract, a party (the lessor) lets a thing for temporary use to another party (the lessee) for a rent over a fixed period when the lessee may use the thing or take the fruits (profits) of such thing. The lessor is obliged to pass the leader thing to the lessee in a condition fit for the agreed use, unless for the customary use.

The lessee is obliged to pay the rent fixed in the contract, or else the amount of rent as usual at the time of conclusion of the contract, taking into account the value of the leader thing and the manner of its use. However, a lease contract is valid even if the contract does not fix the amount of the rent. If a rent is stated in statutory provisions, such regulation applies.

The lease contract terminates upon expiry of the period fixed in the contract, unless the parties agree otherwise. The lease contract concluded for an indefinite period may be terminated only by giving notice of termination, unless the parties come to agreement. In the case of lease of plot of agricultural or forest land, it is required to give a one-year notice of termination, namely, on the first day of October; in the case of other real estate, a three-month notice is to be given; and in the case of movable things, a one-month notice shall apply.

§2. Lease of Flats

118. In the Slovak Civil Code, the regulation of the lease of flats establishes special provisions in relation to the general provisions on a lease contract.

Lease of a flat[24] (apartment) arises on the basis of relevant lease contract under which the lessor lets the lessee use the flat in return for payment of rent, ether for a definite period or without fixing the period of use.

The Slovak Civil Code includes a specific regulation for cooperative flats. In the case of a cooperative flat, the relevant lease contract between the housing cooperative and its member may only be concluded under the terms laid down in the statutes of such cooperative.

The lease of a flat is protected; the lessor may give notice of termination to the lessee only for the reasons established by law (§§710–711, Civil Code).[25]

Unless otherwise provided by the law, rent is agreed on conclusion of the lease contract or a change of rent is agreed during the lease relationship by agreement between the lessor and the lessee. The method of calculation of amounts (charges) for

24. The conceptual feature of flat is purposeful designation of rooms for permanent living in made by a lawful decision of the building department (R 87/2003).
25. Notice of termination is a unilateral act of the lessor against the lessee in which, apart from other requirements, a reason must be given (R 97/1998).

suppliers and services relating to use of a flat and the manner of their payment is laid down in other statutory provisions.

A flat may be jointly leased by two or more persons. Joint lessees shall have equal rights and obligations. In a cooperative flat, a joint lease may only be established between spouses.

If during their marriage, spouses, or one of them, become(s) the lessee of a flat, a joint lease of the flat by the spouses is established. Specific regulation is stated in the case of joint lease of the cooperative flat by the spouses.

The lessee may sub-let the flat to another person (sub-lease) only with a written agreement of the lessor.[26]

The right of lease of a flat can be prescribed by the general rules of prescription (R 31/2010).

Act No. 98/2014 Col. states newly the specific legal regulation of ,'short-term lease of flat'. When the parties agree the contract of short-term lease of flat, they have the choice to use alternatively the text of Civil Code or above-mentioned legal Act. In both legal regulations, the aim of protection of lessee is pursued.

§3. Lease of Non-residential (Business) Premise (Space)

119. Under a specific Act (No. 116/1990 Col.), the lease of non-residential premise (space) is regulated. Under this Act, non-residential spaces are mainly rooms or a suite of rooms designated by the competent building authority for purposes other than housing. A contract of lease of such rooms must be in writing and must contain the object and purpose of the lease, rental amount, method and terms of payment, and the period for which the contract is concluded, unless it concluded for an indefinite period. The lessee may sub-lease such space only with the lessor's consent.

§4. Lease of an Enterprise

120. The Slovak Commercial Code does specifically regulate the enterprise lease as a contract type. Such a contract may only be concluded as an unspecified contract with the respective use of general provisions about the lease contract pursuant to the Civil Code.

§5. Lease of a Means of Transport

121. The essential provision of this contract type stipulates that the lessor obliges himself to leave a means of transport for a temporal use of the lessee and the lessee obliges himself to pay the rental fee. It is a relationship of lease, contrary to the means of transport operation whereby the carrier obliges himself to transport load and to

26. Sub-letting the flat or a part of it without a written agreement of the lessor also gives rise to, apart from the lessor's right to terminate lease pursuant to §711, para. 1, let. (d), Civil Code*, invalidity of the contract of sub-lease pursuant to §39, Civil Code (ruling 1 Cdo 49/2000).

carry out one or more trips for this purpose, and the carrier provides the staff and fuel to the means of transport. This provision determines the fundamental terms of the contract as follows:

- the parties to the contract denoted: the lessor of means of transport and the lessee of means of transport;
- the obligation of the lessor to pass on the means of transport;
- the means of transport denoted which is a matter of interest;
- temporality of the means of transport using;
- the obligation of the lessee to pay the charge for using the means of transport.

For the contract to be valid, written form is prescribed by the Commercial Code.

Any type of a means of transport may be subject matter to lease, the contract may be concluded for a term specified or not specified.

The damages arising to the means of transport are borne by the lessor; the exceptions are the instances when the damage was caused by the lessee or by the persons whom the lessee allowed to use the means of transport involved. A right of the lessor to compensation of damages on the means of transport terminates if the lessor has not demanded this compensation from the lessee within six months after returning the means of transport back. The stipulation on the termination of right is an exception in the Commercial Code (it is a preclusion). The lessee is bound to insure the means of transport only if so stipulated under the contract.

In addition to a possible insuring, it is suitable to consider a possible agreement on maintenance and repairs. If not stated otherwise, the lessee is bound under the Commercial Code to maintain the means of transport at the cost of the lessor in the condition he has taken it over, taken into consideration an ordinary wear and tear. A right to costs incurred to the lessee for maintenance of the means of transport must be claimed by the lessee within three months after their incurring; otherwise, the claim cannot be submitted to the Court, if the lessor objects rightfully that the right was not exercised on time. This term is rather short, as the legislator held that problems in bringing evidence would be frequent if the term were longer.

The right to use the means of transport terminates upon the lapse of term for which the contract has been concluded, or by destroying of the means of transport. It further follows from the law that the contract for a specified time can be terminated by notice. The notice becomes effective after thirty days, unless the means of transport lease contract stipulates a different term of notice, or a later time is stipulated in the notice. The contract may stipulate its possible termination as early as upon submitting the notice.

Chapter 7. Mandate

§1. 'Civil' Mandate

122. Contract of mandate is a contract in which the mandatary obliges himself to procure a thing for the mandator or to carry out some other activity. Significant elements of this contract are 'procuring a thing' and 'carry out other activity'. The object of the contract may thus be extensive, involving a juridical act (e.g., filing a case with a state authority) as well as a factual activity (e.g., auxiliary acts in preparation of a negotiation which is the main object of a contract). Another notion is procuring a thing or other activity for the mandator. This means that an activity in favour of the mandator is involved while satisfying a third party's interests is not excluded (e.g., represented by the mandator). The subject matter of mandate contract is only procuring a thing, not the result of procuring itself (the mandatary is not responsible that after carrying out the act the result failed, for example, after applying for a license the Trade Office did not grant the license). Gratuitousness is not an essential of a mandate contract, neither is consideration.

Contract of mandate is closely related to the institute of agency, namely, in case of agency under procuration.

The contract arises upon agreement of the parties on the subject matter and possibly the remuneration if its providing would not be as of ordinary, namely, in regard to the mandator's profession (e.g., an advocate).

Parties to the contract of mandate are the mandator and the mandatary.

The mandatary is obliged:

- to procure a thing or carry out another activity consistent with the subject matter of contract while bound to act according to his abilities and knowledge;
- to observe the mandator's instructions – he may divert only if necessary for the interests of the mandator and he is not able to obtain his consent on time. Any other diversion from instruction is violation of obligation of mandate and therefore the mandatary is liable for damage that might arise;
- to carry out the mandate in person. If the mandatary entrusts the mandate to a third person, he is liable like as if he carried out the mandate himself. If the mandator agreed to mandatary appointing a deputy or the appointment of the deputy was inevitable, the mandatary is liable merely for faults in selecting a deputy;
- to report completely, if required, about the course of the mandate performance and to transfer all benefits arising from the mandate performed on the mandator;
- to render an account after the mandate performance.

The mandator is obliged:

- to provide the mandatary, if required, with all appropriate means necessary for performing the mandate;
- to reimburse all necessary and beneficial costs incurred to the mandatary even if the result failed to come;
- to recover damage including the faultless one arising in relation to the mandate performance (with the restricted scope in case of an accidental damage);
- to provide remuneration (only if agreed on or if it is common). The mandator is so obliged even if the result failed to come unless procedure failure has been caused by the mandatary's breach of duty.

Legal relationship between the mandator and the mandatary terminates, as appropriate, pursuant to the provision on full agency extinction, that is, by performing the act, revoking the mandate, repudiation by the mandatary or by mandatary's death. Upon termination by repudiation, the mandator is bound to reimburse the mandatary the costs incurred before repudiation, the damages and possibly a part of the remuneration appropriate to the work done.

The Civil Code contains more detailed provisions concerning two special types of mandate contract.[27] First, it is the contract of procuring a thing in which the procurer obliges himself to procure a certain thing. The procurer is entitled to procure the thing also through a third person and the ordering party is bound to pay remuneration for procuring the thing. The other type is the contract for procuring a sale of a thing under which the ordering party acquires the right for the procurer to take from the ordering party a thing intended for sale and take necessary measure for the sale.

The contract for procuring a thing may be concluded in any form, but the procurer must confirm it in writing for the ordering party (including the subject matter, price and date of procuring). The ordering party may rescind the contract of procuring a thing by the time of the procuring itself; however, he must reimburse the beneficial costs and other damages incurred unless the procurer could prevent them to arise. The procurer is bound to observe the ordering party's instructions; he may divert from them only if it is inevitable for the ordering party's interests and if he was unable to obtain his consent on time.

Contract for procuring a sale of a thing must be concluded in writing (otherwise it is void) and contain the following obligatory elements: subject of sale, price for which the thing is to be sold, remuneration to the procurer for the procuring, and a fee to be paid in case of rescission of the contract prior to the time agreed. Right to remuneration arises for the procurer only if the thing entrusted was sold. The contract will be terminated if the procurer does not sell the thing within three months after the day he was entrusted the thing to be sold, unless stated otherwise by the parties. It is common to agree that if the thing is not sold within three months, it will be sold at a reduced price after this time. The Civil Code contains also an important provision on liability for defects of the thing. Not the party ordering, but the sale procurer is liable

27. A contract whose subject matter is, apart from the obligation to procure concluding a contract for someone, also an obligation to make (on the basis of a written power of attorney) legal acts with third persons, or to procure a certain thing or to perform a certain activity, must be considered a mixed one that is adequately regulated by provisions on contract of procuring and provision on contract of mandate (ruling 5 Cdo 65/2003).

to the purchaser for the defects of the thing. Liability involves not only the defects, but also the fact that the thing has properties reported during the sale. The extent of liability is governed similarly by provisions on sale of used things. The Civil Code sale procuring regulation may not be applied for sale of securities. Here special regulation applies as the securities law requires consignment contract provisions under the Commercial Code to be used.

A specific type of contract for procuring is the contract for procuring a tour regulated by §§741–741k, Civil Code. §741b lists mandatory elements of such a contract and other requirements which potentially make the contract voidable.

§2. 'Commercial' Mandate

123. The Slovak Commercial Code has its own legal regulation of contract of mandate.

Under 'commercial' contract of mandate, a mandatary obliges himself to arrange for the mandator, at his cost and for payment, a certain business matter through carrying out juridical acts or through performing other activities and the mandator obliges himself to pay him for it. If arranging the matter is the object of the mandatary's business activity, the payment is deemed to have been agreed on. No written form is prescribed for the contract of mandate.

Fundamental terms of a contract of mandate include:

- the parties denoted: the mandatary and the mandator;
- denoting the subject matter of the contract, that is, arranging certain business matter through carrying out legal acts on behalf of the mandator and on his costs, or through performing other activity at the cost of the mandator;
- payment.

This contract establishes a business contract relationship denoted as relative business, with the exception of contract of mandate for sale of securities, which is an 'absolute' business (*see* above).

Payment, as a fundamental feature of a contract of mandate, is as a rule expressed directly in the contract of mandate by stating the amount of payment. Were it not so and the contract otherwise contains fundamental terms of a contract of mandate, a refutable presumption applies that the payment has been agreed upon in the amount stated by the Commercial Code. If stated expressly in the contract that arranging the matter will be carried out for free and its content would otherwise be quite certain, the contract of mandate would be governed by the Commercial Code which can be concluded as a gratuitous contract.

The contract of mandate differs from the commission contract, the subject matter of which is also arranging a certain business matter by the fact that the mandatary acts on behalf of the mandator while the commission agent acts in his own name. The contract of mandate must also be distinguished from the contract for work. Even though a certain activity of the entity obliged is involved in both cases, its result is not materially tangible in case of the contract of mandate.

The subject matter of the mandatary's activity may be of two types:

- either performing juridical acts by the mandatary on behalf of the mandator (e.g., conclusion of contract, filing complaints in reclamation, representation in court proceedings); or
- in real activity for which authorizing is not necessary (procuring certain information, providing conditions and prerequisites in carrying out certain businesses).

The mandatary is bound to proceed in the given matter exercising reasonable care, and the activity he has obliged himself to carry out in the contract must be according to the mandator's instructions, and with his interests, which the mandatary knows or must know. The mandatary is further bound to inform the mandator of all circumstances occurred in arranging the matter that may cause the mandator's instructions to be changed. The Commercial Code stipulates when the mandatary may divert from the mandator's instructions. The mandatary is bound to arrange personally the matter in question only if so stipulated in the contract. If no such stipulation is included, the mandatary may arrange the matter by entirely or partially employing another person. In such case, he is liable as if performing the obligation himself. The mandator is bound to deliver things on time and information necessary for arranging the business to the mandatary unless it arises from their nature that they are to be procured by the mandatary. When arranging the matter in question a juridical act is to be carried out on behalf of the mandatory and the mandator is obliged to grant on time and in writing the necessary procuration to the mandatary. Issuing the procuration and serving it on the mandatary is common in practice, as it is necessary in all cases when the mandatary is to carry out juridical acts on behalf of the mandator (e.g., conclusion of contracts). If the mandatary is supposed to act on behalf of the mandator, he must be so authorized and the respective authorization may be included in the contract. However, it is more suitable to grant separate and specific procuration. It is not sufficient that the nature of the matter involved requires acting on behalf of the mandator and thus the contract obligation is formulated, not even if the person with whom the mandatary negotiates is aware of the obligation.

The mandatary is bound, without an unnecessary delay, to pass on to the mandator the things he has taken over for him in arranging the matter. The mandatary is liable for damage on the things taken over from the mandator to arrange the matter and on the things taken over during their arranging from third parties, unless this damage could not have been prevented although exercising reasonable care. The mandatary is bound obligatorily to insure the things taken over as stated only if so stipulated by the contract or is specially demanded by the mandator, at the cost of the mandator.

Principle of payment for the contract does not mean that the payment must be stipulated under the contract. If the amount of payment has not been stipulated by the contract, the mandator is bound to pay to the mandatary an amount ordinary at the time of conclusion of the contract for a similar activity carried out by the mandatary in arranging the matter arising from the contract. Unless stipulated otherwise in the contract, principally a right to payment arises to the mandatary when he has carried out properly the activity he was obliged to, regardless of whether it has brought the effect expected, or not.

The mandatary is not liable for breach of obligation of a person with whom he has concluded the contract to arrange the matter agreed, unless he guaranteed in the contract performance of the obligations taken over by other persons in relation to arranging the matter.

Specific manners of an obligation termination arising from a contract of mandate by the mandatary's or the mandator's notice are governed by the Commercial Code. They include automatic termination upon the mandatary's death, if he is a natural person, or by extinction of a corporation that performed the function of mandatary.

Chapter 8. Bailment (Contract on Custody, Deposit)

§1. 'Civil' Bailment

124. Under the Slovak Civil Code, bailment is a legal relationship in which the bailee is bound to take over a thing from the bailor for bailment and to take care of it properly. Legal relationship arises from an agreement on bailment which should contain the clauses on the thing being taken over, on remuneration as a rule, and on the period of the bailment. There is no written form prescribed for bailment. However, it is possible to hand over and to take over the thing by using technical means (left luggage box).

The bailor:

- is entitled to hand over the thing to the bailee to hold it on trust, and the custody must be carried out in the manner agreed, or diligently, if the manner of bailment was not agreed upon;
- is entitled to demand returning the thing at any time unless agreed or evident from the circumstances as for how long the thing should be in bailment;
- is obliged to compensate the loss arising from bailment to the bailee as well as the costs incurred to the bailee in carrying out his duty.

The bailee:

- is entitled to hand over the thing in bailment to another bailee if this option was agreed in the contract;
- is entitled to reimbursement of the necessary costs incurred during the custody of the thing;
- is entitled to a remuneration if agreed, or if the remuneration is consistent with the business of the bailee, or if it is common;
- is obliged to arrange insurance if it is common;
- is obliged to return back the thing to the bailor when required even before lapse of the period of the bailment agreed;
- has the right to return back the thing any time unless the period of bailment is agreed on or is evident from the circumstances.

Both the bailor and the bailee may claim their mutual rights arising from the bailment no later than in six months. The rights become extinct if not claimed within this period. This period obviously does not start before the thing has been returned. Therefore, the period stated does not restrict the bailor's right to demand returning the thing bailed.

Special instances of liability are stipulated as follows:

(a) If the bailee uses the thing bailed or allows another person to use it, or hands it over to another person for bailment without the bailor's consent or unless necessary, or he is delayed in returning it, he is liable for even an incidental damage arising unless the damage would have affected the thing in bailment anyway.

(b) The bailor is liable for the damage arising to the bailee through bailment as well as for the costs incurred to the bailee in carrying out his duty.

Except general grounds for termination of the contract, the following may be applied:

- lapse of time for which the bailment was agreed (if agreed);
- performing the right to demand returning the thing by the bailor even before lapse of the period agreed;
- performing the right to demand returning the thing by the bailor or returning the thing by the bailee, unless the period for bailment has been agreed on or is evident from the circumstances.

§2. 'Commercial' Bailment

125. Contract of bailment is so-called relative business (principally it will arise between business persons, if apparent, regarding all circumstances that they involve their business activities, and further between their entities). No written form is prescribed for this contract (cf. contract of bailment and contract of storage under the Civil Code).

One fundamental stipulation states that by the contract of bailment the bailee obliges himself to take care of a thing he has with him in relation to business relationship with the bailor, free of charge, for the bailor. If not stipulated in the contract whether the thing should be bailed for payment or for free and bailment is not a subject of the bailee's business, an irrefutable presumption applies that the parties have concluded a contract of bailment.

Essential terms of the contract are as follows:

- the parties to the contract denoted;
- the thing to be bailed denoted. As given by law, the bailee must have with him the thing bailed at the time of conclusion of the contract. Moreover, it must be a thing, which he has with him for a specific reason, related to business relationship with the bailor. Only movables may be object to bailment (in relation to securities a specific regulation under the Securities Act applies);
- bailment free of charge;
- obligation of the bailee to take care of the thing;
- temporality of the bailee's obligation.

Comparing the fundamental provision of the contract of bailment and contract of storage it arises that if bailment of a thing is not object to the bailee's business activities, the parties have respectively concluded a contract of bailment. Under the storage contract regulation if bailment of a thing is subject to the storage manager business activities, the parties are deemed to have concluded a contract of storage. This criterion – the subject matter of the business activity – may differentiate the type of contract in question. Significant features of contract of bailment are gratuitousness and the fact that the thing involved is already with the bailee; giving the thing thus must occur prior to conclusion of the contract or no later than upon its conclusion. If the contract performance is gratuitous but essential terms of this contract are not satisfied, this will often be a storage contract under the Civil Code. In addition to the above stated, it is possible to agree on further essentials, like location and time of storage, place and time of releasing the thing and the manner of the cost reimbursement.

The bailee is bound to release the thing bailed to the bailor at the place of bailment intended under the contract, otherwise in its residence or business place or at the place where he operates the bailment. Unless the place of bailment is specified in the contract, the bailee may release the thing to the bailor at any other place as allowed by law.

Even if the term for bailment was agreed on in the contract, the bailee is bound to release the thing without an unnecessary delay after he has been so asked by the bailor. Time of performance is by law generally stipulated in favour of the bailor in this type of contract.

The bailee is entitled to demand the bailor to take over the thing without an unnecessary delay even prior to the lapse of bailment as given by contract, if further performance of the obligations causes the bailee unreasonable difficulties that he could not predict at the time of making the contract. This applies also if a third party demands releasing the thing. The right as quoted is an exception to the general provision of the time in favour of the bailor. The difficulties must be unreasonable, which could not be predicted by the bailee at the time of conclusion of the contract. As for possible demanding by a third party to release the thing, it is of no significance if the third party is so entitled or not. The bailee need not inspect into this situation.

Cases when the time of bailment cannot be estimated are stipulated separately. Unless agreed or arising from the circumstances in conclusion of the contract it is not clear how long the thing should be bailed, the bailee is bound to release the thing to the bailor as soon as the bailor so demands, and the bailor is bound to take over the thing without an unnecessary delay after being called by the bailee. If the bailor has not taken over the thing on time, the bailee may give him an appropriate period of time. After its lapse, the bailee may withdraw from the contract. If he so notified the bailor prior to the lapse of term, he is entitled to sell in a suitable manner the thing at the cost of the bailor or to have the thing stored by a third party at the cost of the bailor. This provision is a measure in relation to general provision of withdrawal from a contract. In violation of the right claim for liability for damages can be considered, satisfying the conditions stated.

A delay in contract of bailment may occur, namely, in connection with giving or taking the thing or the reimbursement costs.

In addition to general grounds, the obligation arising from the contract of bailment is discharged, namely, by performance, which occurs after releasing the thing bailed to the bailor. In business, the contract of bailment is used as an accessory contract type, that is, as a contract arising in relation to another contractual relationship, when in this contractual relationship an obligation of one party arises to keep the thing with it and take care of it (as contained in §526, Commercial Code). Such other contractual relationship may be, for example, contract of sale or contract for work. Contract of bailment may be applied more broadly also in the situations arising within other contracts, when under the Commercial Code a duty to take care of the other party's thing arises to the party.

§3. Storage

126. The contract of storage is stipulated in the Commercial Code. Fundamental provision stipulates that the storage keeper obliges himself under the contract of storage to take over a thing in order to store it and take care of it, and the ordering party obliges himself to pay the storage charges. If not stipulated in the contract whether the thing is to be stored gratuitously or for payment and storage is the storage keeper's object of business activity, the irrefutable presumption applies that the party have concluded onerous contract of storage.

The contract of storage belongs to the so-called relative businesses (*see* above, in Part I). Thus the same storage keeper will conclude a contract of storage under the Commercial Code in one case, and in the other (e.g., with a foundation) a contract of bailment under the Civil Code.

Based on the fundamental provision, the essential terms of the contract are as follows:

- parties to the contract denoted: the storage keeper and the ordering party;
- object of storage denoted – the thing stored, which may be, unlike under contract of bailment, given to be stored only after the contract was concluded;
- agreement on payment – storage charges;
- the obligation of the storage keeper to take over, store and take care of the thing.

Comparing fundamental provisions of contract of bailment and contract of storage, it arises that if taking care of a thing is not the subject matter of business of the keeper, it applies that the parties have concluded a contract of bailment. Provision of the contract of storage stipulates that if care of a thing is the subject matter of business of the keeper, the parties have concluded a contract of storage. This criterion – the subject matter of business – may distinguish the type of the contract concluded. Essential term of the contract is denoting the subject matter of storage by the storage keeper and the ordering party. Unlike the contract of bailment when the thing is given no later than upon conclusion of the contract (it is a thing that the bailee has with him) under the contract of storage the thing can be handed over only after conclusion of the contract. If storing and taking care of things is not subject matter of business of the keeper, essential would be an agreement on payment. A basic feature distinguishing contract of storage from other contract types providing for taking care of things is its nature involving the payment. The manner and time of storage charges payment may be included in contractual stipulations.

Storage contract need not have a written form; however, it is stipulated that the storage keeper is bound to confirm the goods takeover in writing.

The contract may be concluded for a fixed-term for the term of indefinite duration. If the time is not stipulated in the contract, a refutable presumption applies that the contract is concluded for an indefinite period. In such case the ordering party may any time demand releasing the thing and the contract will be discharged upon its return; the storage charges relate only to the real time of storage. If the storage was agreed for a fixed period of time, the ordering party may take over the thing prior to the lapse of the period agreed, but in such case the storage keeper is entitled to storage charges for the whole period of storage agreed on. If the ordering party has taken over the thing before the lapse of the time agreed, he may take use of the term agreed and have the thing stored again, of course, paying to the storage keeper the respective costs.

Liability for delay may arise in relation to taking or giving the thing and the storage charges payment.

The obligation arising from the contract becomes extinct, in addition to general ground, namely, by:

(a) lapse of time stated to the ordering party for giving the thing to the storage keeper (unless agreed otherwise, if the ordering party has not given the thing within six months after making the contract);
(b) releasing the thing stored to the ordering party upon the contract for an indefinite term;
(c) lapse of time agreed for storage;
(d) a one-month notice by the storage keeper. Unless agreed otherwise, the storage keeper is entitled to repudiate the contract after a one-month notice. The term starts running on the first day of the month following the month in which the notice has been served on the ordering party. The fact that the notice term is bound to its serving must be taken into consideration when giving it;
(e) withdrawal from the contract by the storage keeper:

   - if the ordering party has not disclosed a dangerous nature of the thing and there is a serious risk of damage to the storage keeper;
   - if the ordering party owes storage charges for at least a three-month term;
   - if there is a risk of substantial damage to the thing stored, which cannot be prevented by the storage keeper;
   - if the ordering party has not taken over the thing after lapse of the time during which the storage keeper is bound to store the thing.

After withdrawal from the contract, the storage keeper may state a reasonable period of time for taking over the thing with a warning he would sell the thing otherwise. After lapse of this period, the storage keeper may sell the thing in a suitable way at the cost of the ordering party. The storage keeper may deduce storage charges as well as the costs incurred in relation to the sale from the proceeds and must pay the rest to the ordering party without an unnecessary delay.

§4. Commercial Contract on Bank Deposit of a Thing

127. Under a contract on bank deposit of a thing, a bank obliges itself to take over the subject matter of custody from the depositor, to deposit it and to manage it; the depositor obliges himself to pay the custody charges. The subject matter of the contract may only be a thing and it is specially mentioned that securities are exempt from custody. Thus practical use of this contract type is considerably restricted in bank practice. Securities depositing is stipulated in the Securities Act. The contract on deposit of a thing with a bank is an absolute business. No written form of the contract is prescribed.

The bank is obliged to take over the custody of the subject matter and with reasonable care to protect it from loss, destroying, damage, or other impairment. The bank is liable for damage unless it was unable to divert it even by exercising reasonable care.

The depositor is entitled any time to demand from the bank to give him the subject matter of the contract wholly or in part, as well as to deposit it again unless the contract has expired in the meantime. At the time when the item was released to the depositor, the bank has no obligation to protect the item. The depositor is bound to pay the bank for this service the agreed or usual charges.

Termination of the obligation may be initiated by notice at any time; it is effective immediately, whether served by the depositor or by the bank. The obligation terminates also when the depositor has taken over all the things that were in the bank's deposit under the contract, unless he expressed his will for the contract to continue to be effective. When the contract has terminated, the bank is bound to release all the items kept in custody under the contract; the depositor is bound to take them over and to settle the debt for the time of the custody contract. If the depositor has not paid the debt and the bank still retains the subject of custody, lien on the item arises to the bank.

Chapter 9. Accommodation for a Short Term

128. Accommodation is under the Slovak Civil Code a legal relationship in which the accommodator (e.g., an owner or a manager of a hotel) is obliged to provide the ordering person with a temporal accommodation for the time agreed or for the time arising from the purpose of accommodation in the facilities assigned for this purpose (hotel, hostel, lodging house, etc.); and to provide performance related to the accommodation, while the ordering person (the accommodated person) is bound to pay the price to the accommodator within the terms as stated by accommodation rules.

The accommodation is provided under contract, the essentials of which are an agreement of the place and manner of accommodation and stating the period of accommodation. The price will be determined by accepting the proposed price determined by the accommodator as stated in the rules of accommodation.

Regarding the intent to provide temporal (short-term) accommodation, this relationship differs from lease of flats and lease of dwelling spaces in facilities intended for permanent dwelling.

The person accommodated (or ordering) has the following rights and obligations:

- the right to use the rooms reserved for him for accommodation as well as common spaces of the accommodation facility and to use services related to the accommodation;
- the duty to use the rooms reserved for him for accommodation as well as the services related to the accommodation as proper. The person accommodated may not carry out any substantial changes without consent of the accommodator;
- the right to rescind the contract prior to the lapse of the period agreed;
- the duty to compensate the accommodator for the loss incurred by early rescission of the accommodation unless the accommodator could prevent it;
- the duty to pay the price for the accommodation and for the related services to the accommodator within the terms stated by accommodation rules.

The accommodator is:

- entitled to rescind of the contract prior to the lapse of the term agreed if the person accommodated in the facility, in spite of being warned, has grossly violated good morals or has otherwise violated his obligations arising from the contract;
- obliged to hand over the rooms reserved for the accommodation to the person accommodated in a condition suitable for proper use and to provide for him an undisturbed performance of his rights related to accommodation.

Rules of accommodation may contain particulars of the rights and obligations of the contractual parties. To make them part of the contract, it is necessary for the ordering person (the accommodated person) to get acquainted with them upon contracting or to accept them subsequently.

Except for general provisions for liability, the following stipulations apply:

- Liability for damage. Under the provisions on liability for damages caused on the items brought in or deposited, the accommodator is liable for the damages arising on the things brought into the space of accommodation by the person accommodated, or for him.
- The accommodator is entitled to rescind the contract prior to the lapse of the term agreed in case of gross violation of good morals or gross violation of contractual duties even though warned.

General reasons for the contract discharge include mainly the lapse of time for which the accommodation has been agreed. Also the death of the accommodated person is a reason for discharge of the accommodation contract.

The grounds for withdrawal from a contract by both the accommodator and the accommodating party are specifically stipulated. The person accommodated may withdraw from a contract prior to the lapse of time agreed at any time and for any reason; however, he is obliged to compensate the respective loss to the accommodator unless the accommodator could prevent it. The accommodator may rescind prior to the lapse of time agreed if the person accommodated has grossly violated good morals or has otherwise seriously violated his duties arising from the contract in spite of being warned.

Chapter 10. Transportation

§1. 'Civil' Transportation

129. Obligations during transportation secure the needs arising in relation to transportation of natural persons in vehicles, their luggage as well as carriage of goods. Transportation relationship arises between the carrier (the business person carrying out transportation) and the traveller, the sender, and the recipient. The basic distinction of transportation relationships is transportation of persons (transportation of passengers and their luggage) and carriage of goods.

I. Transportation of Persons (Passengers)

130. Transportation of passengers is a service provided to passengers involving in transporting and shipment of the items (travellers and their luggage, including the instances when each is transported separately) by a means of transport to their destination, properly and on time, for a fare stated.

Distinguishing the manner, how a luggage is transported (i.e., together with the passenger and under his supervision or separately from the passenger) is decisive for liability for the damage caused to a thing.

For transportation of persons, it is also significant whether it is a regular or irregular transportation and whether it is carried out either individually or in groups.

Legal relationship in transportation of persons arises by a contract between the passenger who may be any natural person capable and satisfying the terms stated by rules of transport and fares, and the carrier.

Legal regulation of transportation of persons is included in the Civil Code. More detailed rules are given by special regulations, namely, rules of transportation and fares (these regulations become part of the contract for transportation if accepted by the contractual parties). Rules of transportation may under this regulation include stipulation effective in international transportation for the inland transport liability for damages on health as stated by the Civil Code may not be restricted.

Rights and obligations of a passenger:

- duty to pay the fare for the transportation as stated. The amount of the fare is determined by transportation rules or tariffs that also stipulate the instances when the passenger is entitled to transportation free of charge, or to a reduced price;
- duty to pay the price for luggage transportation;
- duty to observe relevant stipulation of the rules of transport and fares for the particular way of transportation and to observe the carrier's instructions (cf. rules of transportation).

Rights and obligations of a carrier:

- duty of care especially for safety and comfort of passenger during transportation and in group (public transportation) to enable them to use social and cultural facilities;
- the duty of care for the luggage (transported separately) to be transported to its destination no later than simultaneously with the passenger;
- the right to sell uncollected items transported under similar conditions as in failure to collect repaired or adjusted things.

Liability for delay under the Civil Code is outlined only when relevant stipulations are contained mainly in the rules of transportation. This applies mainly to regular public transport. In irregular transport, the carrier is liable for delayed transport only if the passengers have suffered damage as a result. The terms and extent of compensation are stipulated under the rules of transportation, too. A claim arising from liability must be claimed against the carrier without delay, no later than within six months. The respective rights become extinct if not claimed within this period. The rights already claimed enjoying a special statute of limitation of one year may not be omitted except the right to recovery of damages in transportation of persons.

The carrier is liable for damage caused on health or luggage transported together with the passenger, or to the things he had on him, under the stipulations on liability for damage caused during the operation of the means of transport. The liability of the carrier for damage occurred during the transportation of the luggage transported separately from the passenger is stipulated under provisions on liability for carriage of goods.

The legal relationship terminates as generally applicable (namely, by performance), the Civil Code contains no specific provisions.

II. Carriage of Goods

131. Carriage of goods is a transportation provided to the consigner involving transportation of a consignment to its destination and its handing over to the consignee. Legal relationship arises between the consigner and the carrier by contract for which no specific form is prescribed. The consigner is bound to confirm in writing the order to the carrier if and when required, and the carrier is obliged to confirm in writing taking over the consignment to the consigner if and when required. The article may be any movable thing if consistent with the terms of transportation rules, that is, capable to be transported. The parties of the legal relationship are predominantly the carrier and the consigner, but it may also be the consignee, unless the consignor and the consignee are the same person.

Legal regulation for carriage of goods is included in the Civil Code. More detailed regulation of carriage of goods is given in special rules, namely, rules for transportation and rates (these rules become part of the contract for carriage if accepted by the parties to the contract). Here the rules for transportation in inland transportation may take over stipulations applicable in international transportation.

The Commercial Code stipulates a similar contractual relationship arising by contract for carriage of a thing and is applied among legal persons. Regardless of the nature of the persons, the stipulations of the Commercial Code for forwarding contract and for the contract for operation of a means of transport may be applied.

Rights and obligations:

(a) of the consigner:

- duty to pay the rate for carriage of the consignment;
- duty to confirm the order of consignment if required;
- right to issue new instruction consistent with the terms stated by rules of consignment.

(b) of the consignee:

- the duty to take over the consignment in its destination, unless done so within six months, the carrier is entitled to sell the item. Rules of transport may state the terms for taking over certain items without the time shorter than six months;
- right to give new instructions to the carrier is granted by the transportation rules and consistent with the terms stated under them.

(c) of the carrier:

- the duty to transport the carriage of consignment to its destination;
- the duty to confirm in writing taking over the consignment if required;
- the duty to carry out the carriage expertly and within the term stated;
- the duty to hand over the consignment in its destination to the intended consignee;
- right to employ also other transporters in transporting the carriage involved;
- right to sell uncollected consignments under the terms similar to those applicable for uncollected repaired of adjusted things.

Liability for damage arising on the consignment transported at the time between its taking over and its handing over, regardless of faultiness, is specifically stipulated under the Civil Code. The reasons for a leeway result from the situation when the carrier is not liable for the damage caused by the consigner or the consignee, faulty article, packaging or cover, special nature of the consignment, or a circumstance that could not be averted by the carrier. The respective reasons may be itemized in rules of transportation. In case of loss or consignment destroying, the carrier is obliged to compensate the price that the lost or destroyed consignment had at the time of being taken over to be transported. The carrier is further obliged to bear necessary costs incurred in relation with the lost or destroyed article. Compensation is preferred unless repair of the thing is reasonable, in which case the cost is borne by the carrier. The carrier is also liable for damages arising from exceeding the delivery term; the terms and remedies are stated by the transportation rules. The carrier is always the liable person, even in cases when other persons transport the carriage. When the transportation is carried out jointly by several carriers as a joint transportation, the transportation rules state which carrier and what terms will be liable for this transport.

Recovery for damage must be claimed against the carrier within six months after the consignment has been handed over to the consignee, or, if the consignment was not handed over at all, within six months after taking over the consignment to be transported. Rights not claimed in fixed terms become extinct.

Discharge of obligations arises under general terms, by performance as a rule. Transportation rules may stipulate some specific ways of discharge.

§2. 'Commercial' Transportation of Goods

132. The Slovak Commercial Code contains a specific regulation of the contract for transportation of goods. The basic provision of this contract type establishes that under the contract for transportation of the goods the carrier obliges himself to the consignor to transport a thing (consignment) from a certain place (place of dispatch) to a certain other place (destination) and the consignor obliges himself to pay the carriage charges. This provision establishes fundamental terms of the contract which are:

- parties to the contract denoted: carrier and consignor;
- denoting the consignment (thing to be transported);
- obligation of the carrier to carry out the transport;
- denoting the place of dispatch and destination;
- the obligation of the consignor to pay to the carrier the charges for the transport carried out, the amount of which need not be agreed under the contract.

Neither the transport deadline nor the recipient needs to be stated under contract. The contract need not be concluded in writing, but the carrier is entitled to demand from the consignor to confirm the transport required in a written transport document and the consignor is entitled to demand from the carrier to confirm in writing the consignment takeover. If special documents are needed for the transport, the consignor is bound to pass them over to the carrier no later than upon passing over the consignment for transport. The consignor is liable for damage caused to the carrier by failure to pass over these documents to him or by the defective content of the documents. Pursuant to §622, paragraph 4, Civil Code, it is not possible for the parties to agree on restriction of the carrier's liability which is established in §622, paragraphs 1–3.

The difference between this contract and other contracts for providing transportation (contract for operation of a means of transport, contract for transportation of a thing, forwarding contract) arises from their fundamental provisions. Under contract for transportation of a thing, the carrier obliges himself to transport the thing himself, while in forwarding contract, the forwarder basically only procures the transport, which will be carried out by another party.

An important role is played by carriage rules that may stipulate in details some aspects of transportation contract, for example, rise of the contract, transportation documents, excluding a thing from transportation, taking over the consignment by the carrier and its passing over to the recipient, the extent of rights towards the carrier and their performing. Relevant is also the stipulation of international treaties, for example, treaties on international transportation, treaty on transportation contract in the international road transportation (CMR), international agreement on transportation of goods on railways (CIM).

The contract parties agree mainly on the application of the relevant carriage charges of the carrier. The carrier is entitled to the charge agreed, or, if not agreed, the charge usual at the time of conclusion of the contract with the regard to the content of the carrier's obligation. The carrier is entitled to the carriage charges after carrying out the transportation to its destination, unless other terms are stipulated by the contract. The carrier is entitled to a prorate charge with regard to the transportation already carried out, if he is unable to complete the transportation due to the facts he is not responsible for.

Carrying out the transportation and choosing the particular type and manner of transportation depend on the content of consignment and its nature. Therefore, the consignor is bound to provide the carrier with the accurate information on the content and nature of the consignment. In case of failure to do so, he will be liable to the carrier for the damage accrued.

For the legal relationship to extinguish, concerning the contract for transportation of a thing, a special manner for the contract to extinguish is stipulated. The contract is terminated if the consignor has not asked the carrier to take over the consignment at the time stated in the contract, otherwise within six months following conclusion of the contract. This manner of termination applies only when the contract contains no other respective stipulation.

Chapter 11. Agency Contracts (Brokerage)

§1. 'Civil' Agency

133. Legal relationship arises between the broker and the prospective client/ party interested in the brokerage contract by which the broker obliges himself to arrange for the prospective client, for remuneration, conclusion of a contract, and the interested party obliges himself to provide remuneration to the broker if the result has been accomplished through the broker's activity. The significant terms of the contract are the object of contract, that is, the arrangement of the broker to conclude a contract, and the remuneration. The amount of remuneration for the broker should be determined in accordance with price regulation. Unlike the previous regulations of brokerage contract, the current provisions restrict brokerage contracts for conclusion of a contract only, namely, the contract for purchase and various contracts for works.

Brokerage differs from mandate mainly by differences in the status of the broker and the mandator in negotiating on behalf of the party interested or the mandatary. Contract of mandate is also an agency agreement and this agreement is not an element of brokerage contract (granting the procuration would have to be made in writing). The brokerage contract is also regulated in a different and stricter way regarding the right to remuneration (commission).

In addition to the basic broker's obligation to carry out brokerage, the parties have the rights and duties as follows:

- the broker is entitled to a remuneration in the amount agreed (under the Commercial Code, the reward must be agreed pursuant to general legal rules under the sanction of voidness);
- the broker is entitled to reimbursement of the costs but only when explicitly agreed. When in doubt, he is entitled for their reimbursement only when an entitlement to remuneration has arisen;
- the broker and the party interested are mutually obliged to disclose all important information related to the brokerage, namely the circumstances that may influence the decision of the party interested to conclude the contract intended;
- the broker is entitled to act or receive anything on behalf of the party interested only if so authorized by being granted procuration in writing (this is acting at the cost of the party interested).

§2. Commercial Agency

134. By a commercial (business) agency contract, the agent as an independent businessperson obliges himself to involve in a long term for the benefit of the party represented in an activity directed to conclusion of a certain type of contracts (businesses), or bargain and agree on businesses on behalf of the party represented and on his cost.

The contract must be concluded in writing. It is not an absolute business and the parties to the contract thus may be mere entrepreneurs under the Commercial Code.

The stipulations of business agency will not apply for:

- the agents whose activities are not paid;
- persons involved in securities exchange or commodities exchange.

Contrary to the brokerage contract, which relates to conclusion of a single specified contract, typical for business agency contract is continuity of the business agent's activities creating a permanent relationship between the business agent and the party represented, however; not an employment relationship. This activity may concern contract of sale, contract for work, or other contracts, but always those contracts involving a certain type of goods or activities, and not all contracts that may be concluded by the particular represented businessperson.

The subject matter of the agent's obligation is searching for the persons interested in doing businesses as specified in the contract. Thus, this activity is of a factitious nature and therefore no legal relationship arises between the agent and the person represented without any other steps taken, as it is so in the contract of mandate between the mandatary and the mandator. If the contract expressly stipulates that the business agent is authorized to carry out juridical acts on behalf of the person represented, that is, to do business in his name, the respective rights and duties are governed by the respective stipulations on the contract of mandate. Without being granted procuration, the business agent is not authorized to do business on behalf of the person represented, receive anything for him, or to carry out other juridical acts. If the contract includes also an authorization to do business on behalf of the person represented, the business agent is bound to do these businesses only according to the terms stated by the person represented, unless the person represented has expressed his consent to another manner of acting.

The business agent is bound to carry out the activity that he has obliged to do, honestly, with reasonable care and bona fide; he is bound to take care of the interests of the party represented, according to the authorization and reasonable instructions of the party represented and to give the party represented the necessary information available. He also informs the party represented on the development in the market and all circumstances important for the interests of the party represented, mainly those related to decision-taking in doing business. If the business agent cannot carry out his activities, he must inform the party represented about it without unnecessary delay.

In the relationship to the business agent, the party represented is bound to act honestly and bona fide; he is bound mainly:

- to provide the agent with the necessary documents related to the subject matter of business;
- to provide the information necessary to perform the obligations arising from the business agency contract, namely within a reasonable time to inform to the business agent that he presumes a significant reduction of activities as compared to what the agent could reasonably expect.

The party represented is also bound to inform the business representative in a reasonable term that he has accepted, refused, or failed to perform the act provided for by the agent.

The business agent may neither inform other persons on the data obtained within the agency without the consent of the party represented, nor use it for himself or for other persons, if contrary to the interests of the party represented. This duty pertains even after termination of the business agency contract.

Unless stipulated otherwise in the Commercial Code, the stipulations on brokerage contract will be applied to the business agency contract. These stipulations imply that, for example, the business agent may not propose the party represented to conclude a contract with a person he is aware of, or should there be reasonable doubts that this person will properly and on time perform his obligations arising from the contract.

The business agent guarantees fulfilling of the obligations by the third party whom the agent proposed the party represented to do business with or in the name of which he has done business on behalf of the party represented, only if he obliged so in writing and if he has obtained a premium for taking over the liability. His rights and obligations are further governed by the stipulations on liability assumption.

Business agent is entitled to a commission, the amount of which is as a rule stipulated in the contract. If not so, the business agent is entitled to the commission as common in the trade usage in relation to the place of his activities and with regard to the type of goods involved in the business agency contract. Were there no such usage, the agent will be entitled to reasonable remuneration, considering all aspects of the acts carried out. Every part of the remuneration, which varies according to the number and value of the businesses, is deemed a part of the commission. In addition to the commission, the agent is entitled also to claim the costs incurred in his activities, only if so stipulated and nothing contrary arises from the contract and when a right to the commission arose to him from the businesses related to the costs. The right to commission and cost reimbursement does not arise when the agent acted in the business as a business agent or broker for the person with whom the party represented and has concluded a contract of the business involved.

Some rights and obligations of the parties to the business agency contract differ according to whether there are non-exclusive or exclusive business agencies.

Exclusive business agency must always be expressly bargained for under the contract, otherwise it is deemed a non-exclusive agency. If exclusive agency is involved, the party represented is bound to employ no other business agent within the territory stated and for the range of businesses stipulated. The business agent is not authorized to carry out to this extent business agency for other persons or to do business at his own cost or another person's cost. Breach of this duty establishes liability for damages, even though not so stipulated under the contract, and either the business agent or the represented parties are by law entitled, depending on the circumstances, to withdraw from the contract. In exclusive business agency, the party represented is entitled to do businesses related to this exclusive agency even without the business agent's cooperation, but the party is bound, unless stipulated otherwise in the contract, to pay commission from these businesses to the agent as if the businesses were done in cooperation with the agent.

Contrary to exclusive business representation in non-exclusive representation, the party represented may authorize also other persons to carry out business agency for him that was agreed on with the business agent, and the business agent may carry out activities he was obliged to towards the party represented, at his own cost or at another person's cost. The business agent obligation terminates upon the term for which the contract was concluded. If the parties are further governed by the contract even after it has terminated, the contract is deemed extended for the term agreed on for the contract, but no longer than six months. If after lapse of this time the parties are still governed by the contract, the contract concluded for a term specified changes into a contract made for a term not specified. If this contract stipulates, or fails to stipulate, the time for which it was concluded, or if a restriction arises from the purpose of the contract, the contract is deemed to be agreed on for the time not specified and may be terminated by notice of either party. The business agent is entitled to a redress in case of the contract termination according to the Commercial Code.

In the business agency contract, it may be agreed in writing that the business agent may not, for a time specified, but no longer than two years after termination of the contract, carry out an activity that was the subject matter of the business agency, or another activity that would be competitive for the business of the party represented, at his own cost or at another person's cost. Competition clause contrary to these terms will be invalid. In case of doubts, the Court may restrict or declare invalid a competitive clause that would restrict the agent more than necessary for the inevitable protection of the party represented.

§3. Business on Commission (Commissionary Agency)

135. This is a specific type of agency contract under the Slovak Commercial Code. Under the basic stipulation of the Commercial Code, a commissionary agent obliges himself to procure a business matter for the principal in his own name but at his cost, and the principal obliges himself to pay him for it. No written form is prescribed for this type of contract. Fundamental parts of a contract with a commissionary agent include:

- parties to the contract: the commissionary agent and the principal;
- subject matter of the contract, that is, procuring a business matter;
- commission agent's acting in his own name but at the cost of the principal;
- payment.

This contract establishes a contractual relationship denoted as a relative business, with the exception of an agreement for procurement of security sale that is deemed an absolute business, while it is not decisive on the part of the contractual parties whether the contract is concluded by business persons or other entities.

In relation to its content, contract with a commissionary agent has a number of identical features with a contract of agency, as its subject is to arrange certain business matters; essential difference is that the mandatary acts on behalf of the mandator while the commissioner acts in his own name. The brokerage contract must be distinguished from that, too, as its feature is not the final arrangement of a matter (e.g., regular conclusion of a certain contract) but only arranging an opportunity for the party interested in making a contract with a third party. This makes it substantially different from a business agency contract under which this activity is permanent.

In arranging the matter the commission agent, while exercising necessary reasonable care, is bound to act according to the principal's instructions, which he may divert from only in cases given by law. He is also bound to protect his principal's interests he is aware of and related to the matter arranged, inform him about all circumstances that might influence changes of the principal's orders, including the duty to inform the principal on arranging the given matters in the manner stipulated in the contract. Unless so stipulated in the contract, he is bound to do so upon the principal's call.

Unless otherwise stipulated in the contract, the commissionary agent is bound to employ also other persons in performing the contract were he unable to perform the obligation himself. However, he is liable for the employed person's performance of the obligation as if he performed it himself.

The matter agreed is arranged by the commissionary agent himself; therefore, he is liable for the contracts concluded in his own name, even though at the cost of his principal. Therefore, no rights and liabilities arise to the principal towards third parties as a result from the commissionary agent's acts. Third parties are in contractual relationship to the commissionary agent only. A special principal's right is the right to demand from the third party, with whom the agent had concluded a contract, to release a thing, or to perform the obligation if the commissionary agent is unable to do so for reasons concerning his person (e.g., a judgment is enforced against him, or he died).

If the person, with whom the commissionary agent concluded the contract, has not performed the contract, the principal may not claim this from the agent. However, under the Commercial Code, he exceptionally has this right, if:

- the commission agent has taken over in writing such an obligation (he guaranteed for the obligation performance by the person, with whom he concluded contract at the cost of the principal); or
- if he disregarded the principal's order concerning the person with whom the contract at the cost of the principal was supposed to be concluded, that is, he selected a person contrary to the principal's orders.

Regarding the essence of contract with commissionary agent, a special stipulation is contained in law involving transfer of title to the things through a sale contract concluded by the commissionary agent in his own name and at his principal's cost. The title to the so-called commissioned goods does not pass on to the agent: the things intended for sale remain a property of the principal and the things obtained by sale directly become a property of the principal upon their passing over to the agent by the third party.

After arranging the matter, the commissionary agent is bound to inform the principal and to submit an account report. The report must contain the person with whom the commissionary agent concluded the contract with the consequences given in the Commercial Code.

The commissionary agent is bound, without an unnecessary delay, to transfer the rights and things obtained in arranging the matter on the principal and the principal is bound to take them. If the person with whom the commissionary agent concluded a contract during arranging the matter breaches his obligations, the agent is bound, on his principal's cost, to demand performance of these obligations, or to pass on to him the respective debts, with the principal's consent.

Even though the contract with the commissionary agent is basically a contract for payment, agreement on the particular payment is not an essential term of the contract. If payment has not been agreed on, the commissionary agent is entitled to a usual payment, that is, in the amount usual at the time of conclusion of the contract. Along with the payment, the principal is bound to reimburse the necessary or useful costs incurred to the agent while performing his obligation.

In order to withdraw from the contract by the commissionary agent or the principal, similar stipulations under the Commercial Code apply as for withdrawal of mandatary or mandator in relation to contract of mandate.

Contract with a commissionary agent is usually concluded in order to procure certain particular matter and the form of this contract is respectively stipulated under the Commercial Code. It is, however, possible for the contractual parties to agree in the contract on a repeated procuring of the principal's matters on the principal's costs by the commissionary agent's own name for a term of indefinite duration. For such instances, the law refers to an appropriate application of the stipulations on commercial (business) agency contract. An appropriate application is related to the fact that the business agent does not act in his own name and thus he may act only upon special procuration granted by the person represented.

§4. 'Commercial' Procurement

136. Under the procurement contract, the agent obliges himself to carry out activities directed to enable the ordering party to conclude a contract with a third party and the ordering party obliges himself to pay the remuneration to the agent. This contract establishes an obligation relationship denoted as relative business, with the exception of securities sale brokerage, contract on issuing securities procured under agency, and contract on returning security brokerage, under which the obligations arisen are deemed absolute businesses. A written form is not prescribed for the contract.

As explicitly stipulated, procurement contract relates to non-recurring, not permanent procuring of the matter under contract. In case of a permanent business activity, it would be a type of business agency contract. Procurement contract must also be distinguished from the commission contract, under which the agent obliges himself, as a rule in his own name and at the ordering party's cost, to carry out certain juridical acts (mainly making a particular contract); while procurement contract obligation in relation to the ordering party is a mere activity directed to enable the contractual party involved to conclude a particular contract. Most frequently it will be a sale contract, but it may be another contract, too.

The mutual duty to inform between the agent and the ordering party is given directly by law involving the circumstances that may be of importance and decisive for conclusion of the particular contract.

Right to commission arises for the agent most frequently only after the contract for procurement has been concluded. The agent principally does not guarantee the performing of obligations of third parties with whom he concluded the contracts in question.

The agent's right to commission is not barred by the fact that only after the contract discharge a contract with a third party is concluded, or the contract related to the agent's activities is performed.

In addition to the commission, the agent is entitled to reimbursement of costs incurred in relation to the procurement only if so expressly stipulated under the contract, and, if in doubts, only if the procurement agent's right to commission has arisen.

If the ordering party so demands, the agent is bound to give him the information necessary to judge credibility of the person with whom the agent proposes the contract to be concluded.

The procurement contract is discharged – unless stipulated otherwise in the contract – if the contract that is the subject matter of procurement has not been made within the time stated in the procurement contract. Unless the time is stipulated in the contract, either party may terminate the contract by announcing so to the other party.

The sub-types of procurement contract specified by law are purchase or sale of securities brokerage contract, contracts on issuing securities under agency, and contracts on returning a security brokerage.

Chapter 12. Bank Businesses

§1. (Bank) Deposits

137. The following principles apply to all kinds of deposit:

- the depositor is entitled to dispose of the deposit, so entitled is also another authorized person in the instances stated by law;
- the depositor is entitled to interests or other property benefits determined by the bank according to the measures taken under special regulations;
- the depositor may bond the payment of the deposit by coding the deposit or by satisfying another condition.

Depositor's Book/Bank Book

138. By the depositor's book, the bank vouches for acceptance of deposit and the book is a proof of its existence. The bank confirms in the deposit book the changes in the amount of the deposit and other facts related to it. Unless a different amount of deposit has been proven, decisive is the note on the depositor's book. Presenting the depositor's book is a condition for disposing of the deposit. In case of loss or destroying the depositor's book, the depositor may dispose of the deposit only if the bank has declared the book redeemed (extinct). After redemption, the bank will issue a new depositor's book to the depositor or pay him the whole deposit, if required.

Certificates of Deposit and Other Deposits

139. Certificate of deposit is a security (being not merely of a legitimating nature), and therefore it must comply with formal requirements prescribed for security1'es. The certificate of deposit must indicate the amount of deposit; it is not possible to withdraw from such a deposit or to deposit additional amounts while the legal relationship is still in duration.

As for other essentials of the certificate of deposit, they are governed as appropriate by the relevant provisions on depositor's books of the Civil Code.

Among other types of deposits, for example, time deposits, prize certificates, etc., can be mentioned.

§2. Deposit Account

140. Under a written deposit account contract, the bank obliges itself to set up a deposit account for the owner and to pay him interests from the money deposited under the Commercial Code. However, the account owner obliges himself to deposit money in the amount stated under the contract to the account thus set up and to authorize the bank to dispose of his money for the term stated. It is an absolute business contract.

An essential part of the deposit account contract, distinguishing it from current account contract, is the owner's obligation to provide the deposit available for the bank's disposal. The owner may repudiate this contract at any time.

§3. Credit

141. Legal provisions for credit contract are given under the Commercial Code. The contract must contain fundamental terms as stated in the basic provision. Under the basic provision, the creditor obliges himself to provide the debtor, if required, with money up to a certain sum for his benefit, and the debtor obliges himself to return the money and to pay interests. No terms for the form of the contract are stipulated.

Fundamental terms of contract are: the creditor and debtor denoted the amount of credit and the debtor's obligation to return the amount of debt and to pay interests. The subject matter is money in the currency stated. The contract is concluded upon the agreement on providing money and not by the factitious providing the money. The parties may determine currency, the subject matter of contract, also in another currency, not only in the Slovak currency (Euro), if it is consistent with the foreign exchange regulations. Unless agreed otherwise by the parties, the debtor is bound to return the money in the currency provided to him, and to pay interests in the same currency.

Credit contracts belong to absolute business. These contracts are governed by the Commercial Code regardless of the nature of the parties.[28] Any person may be a debtor. Difference among creditors is made by the fact that only those of them whose business activity is providing credits may bargain interests for taking over an obligation.

The debtor is entitled to claim right for the money to be provided within the term stated by the contract. If the term is not stated by the contract, the debtor may perform this right by the time the credit providing has been repudiated by either party. Thus, if the term is not stated in the contract, the debtor may perform his right from the instant of conclusion of the contract until the contract notice term.

The creditor is bound to provide the money to the debtor, if so required by the debtor according to the contract, without the time stated by the debtor, or without an unnecessary delay.

If the purpose for the credit utilization is stated in the contract, creditor may restrict providing his money for performing debtor's obligations performance taken over in relation to this purpose. The principle of purpose therefore is applied only if the purpose, for which the credit is to be used, has been stated explicitly in the contract.

After the money has been provided, the debtor is bound to pay interests in the amount agreed on, but no higher than the amount allowed by law or based on law. Unless the interests are stipulated in such a manner, the debtor is bound to pay ordinary interests required for credits provided by banks in the debtor's residence at the time of conclusion of the contract. If the parties bargain higher interests than those allowed by law or based on law, the debtor is bound to pay interests in the amount allowed by

28. The Commercial Code also regulates means ensuring that the credit and its application cannot be excluded by an agreement of the parties (R 11/1999).

law. In doubts, the amount of interests agreed on is deemed bargained for a year's term.

The obligation to pay interests is payable simultaneously with the obligation to return the money used. If the term for returning the money provided is longer than a year, the interests are payable by the end of each calendar year. At the time when the rest of the money provided is to be returned, the respective interests are payable, too. If the money provided is to be returned in instalments, also an interest from an instalment is mature on the day of the instalment payment. The money provided in the way of credit is paid by the debtor in the term agreed on, either in a lump sum, or by several instalments.

Other Commercial Code stipulations apply as optional. This concerns also the possibility for the debtor to return the money sooner than agreed. Unless agreed otherwise, the debtor is entitled to return the money provided prior to the term stated in the contract. The payment term is stipulated in favour of the debtor. If no earlier returning is involved, the debtor is bound to return the money provided within the term agreed, or within a month following the day he was so asked by the creditor.

If the credit is negotiated through a third person, reimbursement for negotiating the credit does not depend on whether or not the debtor actually makes use of it.[29]

§4. Current Account

142. By a written contract for a current account (budget account, business account, and personal account) the bank obliges itself to set up, since the time stated and for the currency stated, a current account for its owner. By creating a current account, a business contract relationship arises between the bank and the account owner, where the account serves as a form of accounting mutual debts and obligations between them. The bank is bound to receive and to record within the assets the money deposits or payment made for the benefit of the account owner, and according to the owner's instructions, it carries out payments and withdrawals of money from the owner's account. The purpose and basic advantage of current accounts is providing non-cash credit transfer. Credit account contract has the nature of absolute business. It must be made in writing.

Fundamental terms of the contract are bargaining the bank's obligation to open a current account for the owner, stating the time since which it has been set up, and the currency of the account. The contract may be repudiated by the owner at any time. The account can be set up for one or more owners and several persons may have right to dispose of the account even though there is a single account owner. The account owner, that is, the party who concluded the contract with the bank, and the parties authorized to dispose of the money in the account (the balance of the account) must be distinguished.

29. Cf. ruling 4 Obo 89/1999 (published in: Zo súdnej praxe, no. 3, 2001, 60).

§5. Traveller's Cheque

143. Traveller's cheque is a security, authorizing the person stated in it to accept the amount stated in it to be paid upon submitting the cheque for payment under the terms stated by the traveller's cheque drawer. Traveller's cheque is an absolute business. However, the regulations governing bills of exchange and cheques according to the bill of exchange and cheque law (Act No. 191/1950 Col.) do not relate to this type of security, as explicitly stated in the Commercial Code. It is a special type of security generally governed by the Security Act (Act No. 566/2001 Col.) having developed in usage as a tool for providing travellers with money in foreign countries instead of cash. It provides reasonable safety to travellers for the case of loss or theft and enables the drawers to reduce the amount of money otherwise necessarily held in foreign currencies.

Cheque drawers are mostly banks, but other entities, too. The duty to pay the respective amount stated in the cheque based on submitting the traveller's cheque is bound to satisfying the terms stated by the drawer.

The person who issued the cheque (the drawer) is bound to repay the cheque or to arrange its payment. Regarding the fact that cheques are mostly used when travelling abroad, in practice traveller's cheques are as a rule repaid by another entity. Traveller's cheques of big banks and prominent cheque companies are ordinarily accepted for repayments by other entities than the drawer (usually banks). These entities repay the respective money, upon the drawer's order, to the authorized person based on an agreement with the traveller's cheque drawer. If such traveller's cheque contains a payment order, it must also contain the person denoted, to whom the order is directed (i.e., the bank carrying out the payment).

Other obligatory elements of a traveller's cheque are:

- denoting that it is a traveller's cheque;
- the company, the drawer's name, his signature, or a sufficient substitution of signature.

A traveller's cheque may be drawn for other than Euro currency, too.

The denoting of traveller's cheque need not be contained in the text.

If the authorized person is not denoted in the traveller's cheque, the person submitting the cheque may demand its repayment. Thus a traveller's cheque has a nature of a security denoting the owner. In submitting traveller's cheques for repayment the person repaying is entitled to demand an identity document of the person submitting it and his signature in the cheque. The repayment must be confirmed by an authorized person's signature.

Agreements on traveller's cheques operations concluded between traveller's cheque drawers and banks or other persons as a rule impose a duty to submit identification documents and signatures attestation, which is a measure against abuse of a lost or stolen cheque.

Chapter 13. Insurance

144. The purpose of insurance is to secure natural or legal person for case of accidental events by providing them the right for a payment to cover the loss arising as a result of such events.

Every such event is deemed accidental that is considered by the insurance parties as possible to occur; however, at the time of insurance they do not know that it will happen, or whether it will happen at all (e.g., flood, a motor vehicle crash, fire, injury to a natural person). If it is an event involving human life or its length, also such an event is deemed accidental that is presumed by the parties as inevitably occurring, but at the time of insurance negotiations it is not possible to state when this may happen, or whether it will happen at the time for which the insurance was arranged (e.g., the death of a natural person).

Parties to the legal relationship are the policyholder (the insured person, insurant) and the insurer.

With regard to plurality of insurance companies (underwriters), the significance of general insurance terms making part of insurance contract has been growing. General insurance terms contain, namely, specification of the event from which the right to the reimbursement in favour of the insurant arises, assessing the respective amount, reimbursement payment term, assessing the manner and amount of payment, the manner how the insurant in case of insurance of persons shares the profit with the insurance company, if so stipulated under the insurance contract. It is possible to divert under the insurance contract from the insurance terms only in the instances as specified, in other cases if it is in favour of the person insured.

Insurance rules are stipulated mainly in the Civil Code. More detailed are insurance terms that may be diverted from in the insurance contract only in cases specified by them.

Types of Insurance

145. The Civil Code distinguishes insurance according to the legal ground of its rise into:

- contractual insurance;
- statutory insurance.

Contractual insurance is a more common type. Contractual insurance may be also such for which the obligation to conclude insurance contract is given by law – an obligatory contractual insurance. Statutory insurance arises directly under law as a result of the fact stipulated by legal rule.

Another classification is based on the different subject matter:

- insurance of property against loss, damage, theft or other damages that may occur;
- insurance of persons for cases of bodily harm, death, life insurance for attaining certain age or for the case of another insurance event;

- insurance of liability for damage caused to life, on health or on a thing, or for another property damage;
- insurance of legal protection.

Insurance of several types as named is possible under a single insurance contract (e.g., joint insurance). It applies for all types of insurance that the respective juridical acts must be made in writing unless provided otherwise by statutes.

Insurance Contract (Policy)

146. Insurance contract is a bilateral juridical act between the insurant (policyholder) and the insurer (underwriter) on providing insurance protection. Under the contract, the insurer obliges himself to pay the amount agreed, if the event named has occurred during the insurance relationship and the insured person obliges himself to pay the insurance premium as agreed.[30] The contract is concluded at the instant when the person proposing receives the notification of acceptance of his proposal. The proposal of an insurance company may also be accepted by paying the premium in the term stated. The insurer will hand over the form of policy to the insurant as a written confirmation of the conclusion of insurance contract. If the policy has been lost or destroyed, the insured will issue the copy of the policy to the insured at his request and cost.

The insurance contract may be concluded also in favour of a third person. It means that the contract is concluded between the insurer and the insurant in favour of the third person insured. For such a contract general provisions for contract in favour of a third person apply while the consent of the person involved may also subsequently be granted in performing the rights arising from the insurance event.

By conclusion of insurance contract, rights and obligation for the respective parties arise. The insurance company is entitled, namely, to receive policy premium, and it owes the duty to perform, arising on the first day after conclusion of the contract, unless agreed otherwise by the contractual parties.

The insurant (policyholder) is obliged to pay the premium either periodically in the term as agreed (common premium) or to pay the total insurance amount for the whole period of time agreed (lump insurance).

The person whose property, life, health, liability for damage is insured by insurance contract, is entitled to demand reimbursement arising when the event to which the rise of the insurer's duty to pay reimbursement is related has occurred (insurance event occurrence).

The insurant is bound to observe the obligations as agreed or as given by law in order to prevent the extent of the insurance event to grow. The insurant is bound, without a delay, to inform the insurer in writing about the insurance event occurrence.

An important principle is that insurant is entitled to recovery of damages caused by insurance event against another; this right will pass over to the insurer up to the

30. If an insurance contract that includes insurance terms refers to non-existing parts of general insurance terms, the contract is deemed uncertain and non-understandable, hence void pursuant to §37, Civil Code (R 48/2000).

amount of the reimbursement provided to him by the insurer assignment of claim (*ex lege*).

The insurant has to take due care to prevent the insurance event from occurring. In case of violation (knowingly or as a result of intoxication), the insurer is entitled to reduce the reimbursement as appropriate.

Termination of insurance arises by termination of the legal relationship occurring through:

- notice of termination of the contract that must be made no later than six weeks before the lapse of insurance term, which refers to the insurance for which common premium has been taken out. The insurance becomes extinct by the end of the insurance term;
- notice (agreed by the parties beforehand) of termination within two months after conclusion of the agreement. The notice term is eight days and the insurance terminates upon its lapse;
- failure to pay premium for the first insurance term or a lump insurance within three months. The insurance terminates upon lapse of these terms;
- failure to pay premium or its part for another insurance period within one month since being served a written demand. The demand of the insurer includes a notice that the insurance will end if not being paid;
- withdrawal of the insurer from the contract if information duties required by the insurer have been knowingly breached and the insurer would not make the insurance contract if the questions were truthfully and completely answered; this right may be exercised by the insurer within three months since the day he found out such a fact, otherwise the right extinguishes;
- denial to pay reimbursement, if the insurer, only after the occurrence of insurance event, has learned that it was caused by facts that were held back from the insurer when concluding insurance contract and that were material for conclusion of the contract.[31]

Insurance of Property

147. The insurant is entitled upon property insurance to demand reimbursement in the amount as given by insurance terms, if the insurance event involves the facts relevant for the insurance. So-called multiple insurance contract may be concluded.

Insurance of Persons

148. The insurant is entitled, in case of an insurance event (physical harm, living up to certain age, death, etc.), to demand the reimbursement paid by the insurer as agreed or a revenue/pension to be paid or a benefit as stated.

31. If an insurance is ended because the one-off insurance premium has not been paid within the period stipulated in §801, Civil Code, the insurer is entitled to claim from the person who made the insurance contract with him a proportion of the one-off insurance premium for the period preceding the ending of insurance (ruling 1 Obpj 1/2005).

Liability Insurance

149. It is a liability insurance of the insurant involving paying compensation for damages arising in cases as stated towards another person.

Insurance of Legal Protection

150. The basis of this insurance relationship is the insurance where the insurer undertakes to reimburse the expenses of the insured for exercising his right to the extent determined in the insurance contract and to provide services directly connected with this insurance under the conditions agreed in the contract.

Chapter 14. Civil Partnership

151. Partnership of persons arising upon a contract concluded according to Part 8, Head 16 of the Civil Code differs from interest association of juridical (legal) persons as well as from civic association on associating of citizens, as later amended. The partnership contract is a contract under which several persons associate in order to contribute jointly to accomplish economic purpose. This partnership is not a legal entity. Thus the respective rights do not arise to the partnership as such but to its members.

Essentials of partnership contract are:

- partnership of persons (without any restrictions as to the number of members; these can be both natural and juridical persons, persons both involved and not involved in business. However, if the partnership has been founded for the purpose of conducting business, its members may only be those authorized to carry out business);
- joint contribution (may involve both property contribution and personal activities);
- restricting the purpose as taken out (maybe both occasional and permanent ones).

No Special Form of Contract Is Prescribed by Law

152. Each participant is bound to develop activities in order to accomplish an economic purpose consistent with the manner stated in the contract and to refrain from any activity that might make accomplishment of this goal impossible or impaired.

According to the nature of contribution (property or work contribution), the members have the following rights and obligations:

- The member is obliged to provide property values for the purposes of the partnership by the time stated under the contract, otherwise without any unnecessary delay after conclusion of the contract. The money provided or other things stated in kind are in a joint ownership of all members in respect to the portion of their own contribution. Contribution can be made through notification on its separation from other property of the member or by handing over to the authorized member. The single things stated remain in the ownership of the member and are used free of charge by all participants. Unless provided otherwise under contract, the contributions of all members are presumed equal.
- The property obtained in performing joint activities becomes joint property owned by all members. The shares of this property are equal, unless stated otherwise by contract.
- The members are jointly and severally liable to third persons. As a rule, the members decide on arranging common matters unanimously. However, they may agree that certain things, or all of them, will be decided on by majority vote, and in this case, each member has one vote while the amount of his share is not decisive.

An agreement is possible under which disposal, of certain things will be delegated on certain members. Then the right of each and every member, including those who do not perform administration, must be observed, to obtain information on the economy of the partnership. A contract that would exclude this right or by which a member would waive this right will be void.

The members are jointly and severally liable for breach of obligations.

The Civil Code stipulates, not very certainly, liability of parties in such a manner that the party, who quit or has been excluded is not relieved from the liability for the obligations arising from the activities of the partnership that arose by the day he left it or was excluded (the uncertainty lies in the application of an active concept of liability).

Extinction of partnership is not provided explicitly. However, it is evident from the nature of the contractual relation that it terminates mainly by fulfilling its purpose and lapse of the term for which the partnership was established. Of course, an agreement of members to wind up the partnership is also possible. For this instance, the Civil Code stipulates that the members are entitled to demand the return of the values provided for the partnership activities. Parties settle the property obtained by their common activities within the partnership in the manner stated in the contract. Unless the manner of settlement has been contractually specified they will settle by equal shares. It is a winding up of a partnership, and it will apply also to other cases of partnership extinction.

Except absolute extinction of partnership, also termination of someone's party membership must be considered, that is, termination of membership. This may occur by quitting or excluding, or by death (as well as by extinction of a juridical person).

Basically, any member may quit at any time. However, he may not quit at the time unsuitable and at the cost of the other members of the partnership. This restriction does not apply if the reason for quitting is serious; in such case, quitting is possible at any time regardless of whether term of notice has been taken out. In other cases, notice term is to be respected. By quitting, the legal relationship of the member in the partnership contract is revoked and he must receive back the things brought to the partnership. He will be paid up in money corresponding to the state of the property share corresponding to the state on the day of his quitting.

Excluding is a decision taken by all other members of the partnership unless stated otherwise by the contract (e.g., majority decision). However, a member may be excluded for serious reasons only. After excluding, the member property settlement must be carried out according to the same principles as in the case of quitting the partnership.

If a partnership member dies and unless the contract contains the respective provisions that his heirs take over his place, his membership in the association should be deemed extinct. This question is not explicitly regulated by law.

153 – 153

Chapter 15. Silent Partnership

153. Silent partnership is regulated in the Commercial Code. Under a silent partnership contract, a silent partner obliges himself to provide for the businessperson a certain investment and to participate in his business activities, and the business person obliges himself to pay him certain part of the profit – after deducing the obligatory allotment to the reserves fund, if the businessperson is bound to create this fund – corresponding to the investment of the silent partner in the results of the business. In the silent partner contract, the extent of the silent partner's participation in profits and losses must be agreed on equally. The contract is an absolute business and must always be concluded in writing. Essential terms of the silent partnership contract are stating the investment to be deposited by the silent partner and stating the part of profit related to the silent partner's share as the result of business activities which the businessperson obliges himself to pay to the silent partner.

By conclusion of the contract no legal person, for example, a corporation is created but an obligation relationship between the silent partner and the given businessperson is established. Any person (a natural person or a legal person), regardless of whether an entrepreneur or not, may be a silent partner. However, the contract party to a silent partner must be a businessperson under the Commercial Code.

As implied in law, a silent partnership contract is always concluded by the businessperson and one silent partner. This does not exclude conclusion of several silent partnership contracts with several different silent partners, among whom no relation similar to the relationship of business partners arises. If the business concluding the silent partnership contract is a limited liability company or a joint stock company, the approval of such contract and the respective changes will be granted by the general meeting.

The investment of a silent partner may comprise a certain amount of money, a certain thing, a right, or other property value usable in business activities. Silent partner is bound to give the subject matter of investment to the businessperson or to enable him its utilization in business at the time agreed or otherwise without an unnecessary delay after conclusion of the contract. Unless stipulated otherwise in the contract, upon taking over the thing the businessperson becomes its owner; the exception is real property. If real property is subject matter of investment, the businessperson is entitled to use it for the time of the existence of the contract. If the subject matter of investment is a right and the contract does not stipulate otherwise, the businessperson is entitled to exercise it during the time of the contract existence. Thus monetary investment and an investment by a thing increases the given business person's assets and become part of its business assets. If the investment involves a right to use a thing, then during the time of the contract in effect the silent partner may not deal with the investment, even though he remains its owner.

The silent partner is entitled to have access to business documents and account records related to the business he participates in and is entitled to demand a copy of annual balance accounts. Thus, it implies that silent partner does not participate directly in business activities and therefore has no influence on decision-taking in business matters. The annual final account is a basis for calculation of the silent partner's share and therefore he has the right to demand its copy. The right to the share of the profit, for whose calculation the final account is decisive, arises to the silent partner within thirty days after completing the final account. If the businessperson is a legal entity, the term starts running after approving this final account according to the respective Articles of Association, deed of partnership, or law. The silent partner is not bound to return the share received in case of a later loss. The law further stipulates that the silent partner's investment will be reduced by the portion of the loss suffered. In the years to come the reduced investment will be increased by the profit share and the right to the share in the profit arises to the partner after attaining the original amount of investment. The silent partner is not bound to provide additional investment in case of loss in business activities and he takes part in the loss only up to the amount of his investment. Therefore the time, during which right to the share in profit arises to the silent partner, differs, depending on whether the businessperson given is a natural person or a company. Principally the right arises upon the final account and it is an independent right. Therefore, in case of profit share in one year and a loss in the following year the partner is not bound to return the profit share received. If during the following years only losses occurred, the silent partner is not bound to provide additional investment. The contract terminates if the whole of his investment has been exhausted.

Rights and obligations towards third parties in business principally arise to the businessperson. Therefore, it is only the businessperson who acts outwards and rights and obligations arise to him. However, under law a silent partner guarantees for the businessperson's obligations in the two following cases:

- if his name is contained in the business company of the businessperson; or
- if he announces the person, with whom the businessperson has been bargaining a contract that they are in business together.

Were the name of the silent partner stated in the business company of the businessperson without his consent, he may claim protection in court; in the other from the above-stated cases, it will always be the result of a silent partner's act.

The silent partner's participation terminates in cases stated under the Commercial Code. The contract may be concluded both for a fixed or unspecified time. Unless another notice period has been specified in the contract, it may be repudiated no later than six months before the end of calendar year. Before lapse of the time stated for the silent partnership duration it is possible, for serious reasons, to demand the Court to cancel the obligations arising from the contract. This possibility applies also for a contract concluded for the time not specified. After the contract termination, that is, by extinction of the silent partner's participation by law, or after termination by a court decision, a settlement must be made with the silent partner. The businessperson is bound to return the silent partner his investment increased or decreased by his share in the results of business activities.

Unless the provisions of the Commercial Code imply otherwise, the silent partner has a similar legal position in regard to his investment as a creditor in regard to the debt owed to him; but he is not entitled to demand returning his investment prior to the termination of contract.

Chapter 16. Private Annuity

154. Legal relationship arises under the Civil Code between the person entitled and the person owing upon private annuity contract. This contract provides ground for the person entitled to be paid a pension for life or for a term of uncertain duration (e.g., during illness or for a temporary period of disability). It is so-called provisory pension supplementing benefits provided from pension insurance.

The person entitled may only be a natural person, which is evident from the nature of the right arisen; the person owing may be both a natural and a juridical person.

For pension contract a written form is prescribed, failure to observe it makes the contract void.

Basic right of a pensioner (the person entitled) is the right to payment of the pension benefits as agreed. This right is of personal nature, non-transferable, does not pass on to heirs. Benefits may be both monetary and in kind. They are payable in the terms agreed. However, personal nature of this right does not exclude to transfer upon another the benefits already payable.

The person owing is entitled to require payment, as a rule while the pension contract is being concluded (usually this payment means to turn over some property value) but only if it was agreed on.

Legal relationship becomes extinct first of all by lapse of time for which the contract was taken out, and possibly upon the term of cancellation coming up. The extinction of the legal relationship arises no later than upon the death of the person entitled as it is linked with this person.

Chapter 17. Wagering (Betting) and Gaming

155. Neither bet nor game is stipulated under the Civil Code, only some of their legal consequences are commented on. Therefore, it is necessary to rely on their general features when characterizing them.

Wagering may be one-sided or two-sided. A one-sided bet is a contract in which one party promises performance to the other party in the case that from the opposite assertions of the parties the assertion of the promising party proves false. Double-sided bet is a contract in which both parties promise one another the performance for the case that their respective assertions will prove false. Thus the essentials of wagering (wagering contract) are opposite assertions of the parties on whether a certain fact has existed, exists, or will occur. The respective questionability must be based on lack of knowledge concerning this fact by the parties.

Gaming may be one-sided or two-sided, too. In a one-sided gaming, one party promises the other a performance dependent on the result of a game that is played according to certain rules. It is basically the same for the two-sided gaming, except that more than one party will actively take part in the game. Unlike wagering, gaming presumes certain activity of the parties (physical or mental, typically a sport). Gaming will be valid under the condition the rules stated or agreed upon have been observed.

Criminal law imposes sanctions for running monetary or other similar type of gaming or wagering, the rules of which do not guarantee equal opportunities to win for all participants.

A lot as well as a letter, in which a performance is promised in case the number borne by the lot will be drawn according to certain rules, is considered in a similar manner as wagering or gaming. Lots are also common nowadays where winning is secured in another way, for example, wipe-of lots.

The Civil Code deems the claims to winnings in wagering and gaming as natural obligations except in case of an enterprise run by the state or permitted by the state. Similarly to the provisions under §455, the Civil Code declares that winnings in bets, games, and debts from loans provided knowingly for wagering or gaming cannot be claimed. These are the so-called non-actionable debts (natural obligations). These debts cannot be effectively secured, either. Still, these debts are effective and therefore voluntary performance is possible.

Chapter 18. Public Competition

156. Public competition (competitive bidding) arises based on a one-sided non-addressed juridical act by which a natural or juridical person declares competition for a certain work or performance, for which it promises a reward.

Public competition as a unilateral juridical act is effective by its declaring as this juridical act is not addressed to a certain group of subjects. General terms of the juridical act must be met while from the specific nature of competition it follows that this juridical act must further contain:

- exactly defined subject matter and terms of competition;
- prize and other competition terms;
- declaration regarding who and under what rules will evaluate the fulfilment of satisfying the terms of the competition;
- defining who and under what conditions may take part in the competitive bidding.

A form of public notice is prescribed for declaration of competition in order to guarantee that the public will be informed about the content of the competition.

Legal relationship between the declarer of the competition and the competitor will arise only if the competitor expresses lawfully his will to take part in the competition.

It is necessary to distinguish competition under the Civil Code from public tender regulated by the Commercial Code.

By declaring competition, the declarer is bound and as a result he acquires rights and obligations: he is obliged to provide the prizes declared by the competition to those who, according to the evaluation, have satisfied the requirements of the competition stated for the prizes to be granted. If the result was accomplished through activities of several competitors, the prize will be divided according to the share of each of the participants' contribution unless another manner was announced. The prize is evidently presumed by law to be a divisible performance. Eventual disputes are resolved by Court.

The competitor, who applied for the competition, is not bound to take part in the competition. He is obliged to provide the results of his activities to the declarer only when this follows from the competition terms or from the nature of the matter.

Competition may be cancelled for serious reasons only, and cancellation must be carried out in the same manner as the competition was declared, or in another, equally efficient manner. A substantial change of the competition content is deemed its cancelling and declaring of a new competition at the same time.

The declarer is liable for damage arising by breach of his legal obligation under general provisions. In relation to competition, the right to compensation is stipulated, which, of course, has not the features of liability for damages. If competition has been cancelled, the declarer is bound to provide appropriate compensation to the competitors who have met the terms, either fully or in part, of the competition prior to its cancellation. Also the declarer is bound to notify the competitors to claim compensation in case of the competition cancellation.

Chapter 19. Public Promises

157. Public promise (covenant) is a one-sided juridical act in which it is promised by public declaration that a reward will be paid or other performance will be provided to the persons not defined in case of meeting the terms stated in the promise. Public promise may be made by a natural person or an artificial legal person.

A contractual relationship may arise from a public promise, however, not immediately after publishing it. Legal relationship arises only when a person has started executing of the performance demanded, or only after meeting the terms stated in the public promise.

In the newly formed legal relationship, the person who announces promise is bound to grant the reward promised. The Civil Code stipulates for this instance that the prize will be granted to the person who is the first in fulfilling the public promise terms. The terms may, however, modify the principle so stated.

If several persons have fulfilled the promise terms at the same time and it follows from the content of the terms that the prize is to be granted to a single person only, the prize will be divided among them equally.

Chapter 20. Package Tours (Travel Contract)

158. Legal relationship arises between the travel agent and a traveller on the basis of a travel contract (a special type of the contract for work). Based on this contract, the travel agent obliges himself to provide the traveller with a tour and the traveller obliges himself to pay the price agreed. The tour is understood as a combination of at least two of the following items, sold or offered for sale at the overall price, and the service is provided for a period longer than twenty-four hours, or if it includes an accommodation overnight:

- transport;
- accommodation (lodging);
- other services for tourists that do not supplement transport or accommodation and are a significant part of the tour.

Travel contract has a prescribed form in writing and one copy must be handed over to the traveller. Contracting process has certain specifications as under the Civil Code the proposal for travel contract is submitted by the travel agent. Travel contract must contain the essentials prescribed, first of all contractual parties, specification of the tour mainly by the date of its commencing and termination, listing all services for the tourists to be provided and the price of the tour, including the schedule of payments and the amount of down payment. If the travel contract fails to contain all these elements, it will be void. Travel contract must also contain further elements: for example, enforcement of claims arising from breach of liability of the travel agent, the amount of settlement, etc. Absence of further elements is sanctioned by the contract being voidable.

The extent of rights and obligations is determined first by fundamental parts of travel contract. Among other rights and obligations, the following may be mentioned:

- the right of the travel agency to increase unilaterally the price of the tour if this option has been agreed on but the price of the tour must not be unilaterally increased within twenty days before the beginning of the tour;
- the duty of the travel agency to provide the customer with further detailed information in writing no later than seven days before commencing the tour;
- the right of the travel agency to propose the customer a change of contractual terms including the right of the customer to accept the change or to withdraw from the contract;
- the right of the customer to substitute persons;
- the right of the customer to withdraw from the contract;
- the right of the travel agency to withdraw from the contract consistent only with the reasons as stated;
- the duty of the travel agency to pay the fine to the customer in case of the tour cancellation;
- restitution duty of the travel agency and the duty of the customer to pay settlement to the agent after withdrawal from the contract;

- set of obligations concerning securing a substitute performance or removing unfavourable effects caused by the circumstances from the outside.

Regarding the breach of rights and obligations of the tour participants (both the customer and the travel agent), usual liability claims arise (liability for delay, liability for damage, and liability for defects). They are specified as follows:

- liability of the travel agent for breach of duties regardless of whether these duties are to be performed by the travel agent himself or by other suppliers of services provided within the tour;
- the term for claiming the rights with the travel agent – both the term of order and preclusion term; for claiming rights the law stipulates a minimum preclusion period of three months since the end of the tour or, if the tour did not take place, since the day when the tour was supposed to end according to the contract;
- leeway reasons as stated in favour of the travel agent as well as leeway for general liability for damage;
- limitation of compensation for damage.

Legal relationship becomes extinct in an ordinary manner of termination of contractual relationship, namely, by performance.

The Civil Code specifies the termination of legal relationship based on withdrawal from the contract both by the customer (distinguishing the withdrawal consequences and according to the reasons) and on withdrawal by the travel agent (as a consequence of a tour cancellation due to the failure to gain the minimum number of the customer or due to breach of duties on the part of the customer).

Chapter 21. Contract for Operation of a Means of Transport

159. Fundamental provision of this contract type establishes that under the contract for operation of a means of transport the operator obliges himself to transport a shipment denoted by the party ordering; and for the purpose to carry out one or more trips denoted in advance, using the means of transport in question; or during the term agreed to carry out trips as denoted by the ordering party and the ordering party obliges himself to pay the charges. Contrary to the contract for operation of a means of transport, in case of lease contract for a means of transport there is only a lease without providing the personnel, fuel, and an obligation to carry out one or more trips. In another contract type concerning forwarding – a forwarding contract – there is only an obligation to transport a thing. Fundamental terms of the contract are:

- parties to the contract denoted: operator of the means of transport and the party ordering the operation of a means of transport;
- the obligation of an operator to transport a shipment;
- denoting the means of transport;
- denoting the trip to be carried out by the means of transport, or the time, during which the means of transport is to transport the consignment;
- obligation of the ordering party to pay for the transport.

The contract must be concluded in writing; it is an absolute business.

The respective Commercial Code provisions concern contract for operation of any means of transport that is special for operation of ships only and for the cases when the shipment is taken over by a ship operator. It stipulates that if under the contract the ship operator takes over the shipment to be transported, the stipulations dealing with the forwarding contract will be applied as appropriate, if so allowed by the nature of the contract for operation of a means of transport.

Chapter 22. Contract for Inspection Activities

160. By the contract for inspection activities, the inspector obliges himself to ascertain impartially the state of a thing or to test results of an activity and to issue a respective evaluation, and the ordering party is bound to pay him a fee. There is no written form prescribed for the contract and it is an absolute business. Fundamental terms of the contract are:

- an obligation to ascertain impartially a state of a thing or to check result of an activity;
- issuing respective attestation;
- payment.

An essential feature of this contract is impartiality as under a mandatory provision of the Commercial Code the inspector is bound to inspect in an impartial manner and to describe the state ascertained in a respective attestation certificate. The provisions of a contract in question prescribing to the inspector the duties that might influence impartiality of the inspection or correctness of the attestation certificate are deemed invalid by law from the very beginning.

The inspector is bound to exercise reasonable care in the manner stated under the contract, in the extent and manner usual in similar inspections. Further, he is bound to carry it out, unless stipulated otherwise in the contract, without an unnecessary delay, in the place where the subject matter of inspection is placed, as given in the contract. Unless the place is determined in the contract, the ordering party is bound to inform the inspector in time about the place and time of the inspection to be carried out.

The right to payment of fee bargained arises to the inspector after complete fulfilment of his duties, for example, following an inspection and a respective attestation certificate issued. If the payment has not been agreed upon, the payment will be as usual at the time of conclusion of the contract, with regard to the subject matter, extent, manner, and place of inspection. In addition to the bargained, or usual, payment, the ordering party is bound to pay the inspector also the necessary and reasonable costs arisen during inspection, unless they are apparently included in the payment of the fee. If the inspector has evidently not carried out the inspection properly, right to payment of charges and the costs does not arise, and unless stipulated otherwise under the contract, the ordering party is entitled to withdraw from the contract after the terms stated have lapsed. Failure to carry out the inspection within the term stated is deemed a fundamental breach of contract.

Under a mandatory provision, carrying out an inspection does not concern legal relationships between the party ordering and other (third) parties, namely, between the parties to or from whom the subject matter of inspection comes.

If the inspector breached his obligation to carry out the timely inspection and while exercising reasonable care, that is, as proper, and damage arose as a result, he is liable for damage under general provisions on compensation for damage. If the subject matter of inspection is quality and quantity of goods, the inspector's liability for compensation of damages is restricted under special regulation as follows: the inspector is bound to compensate damage arisen by breach of duty to carry out the inspection properly only if the damage cannot be made up for by performing the claim of the ordering party in relation to the person liable for the given faulty performance, which is subject to inspection agreed upon between the ordering party and the inspector.

Chapter 23. Quasi-contracts

§1. Obligations Arising from Unjustified Enrichment

I. General Outline

161. Obligations arising from unjustified enrichment present a special group of obligations that are not due under a contract.

General prerequisites for the unjustified enrichment obligations to arise include mainly the fact that a property benefit – enrichment – was obtained by the party not entitled. Enrichment may be of a various nature, for example, performance in rem, monetary performance, the benefit of using another person's thing, or from performances provided in favour of the enriched person; however, enrichment must always be of a property value with the possibility to be objectively expressed in money. In the property sphere of the person enriched, it will be expressed either in increasing his property (direct enrichment), or in the fact that his property has not decreased, although in fact it justifiably should have (the so-called indirect enrichment). One person must get enriched at the expense of another, which means that enrichment of one party is simultaneously a detriment of the other one.

The grounds of unjustified enrichment and the corresponding detriments may involve an act of the person enriched (sometimes an illegal act), an act of the aggrieved party, or common conduct of both parties. It may also be an act of a third party, or an event. An event may induce unjustified enrichment indirectly, too, if performance of a party to a contract becomes impossible as a result of an event, while the other party has already fulfilled its obligation. Here obtaining unjustified enrichment is not a direct consequence of an event but the result of the termination of a legal reason (extinction of obligation due to impossibility to perform).

Enrichment must be unjustified. The cases when a certain property benefit can be deemed an unjustified enrichment are expressly stipulated by the Civil Code. In addition to these special cases, the Civil Code contains a general provision under which 'he got enriched unjustifiably at the expense of another must give up the enrichment'. There is a prevailing court practice under which particular stipulations defining enrichment basically define unjust enrichment according to the law and thus the right to have it given up arises only in the cases listed by law.

The provision on unjustified enrichment under the Civil Code will also apply to the relationships provided under the Commercial Code.

II. The Obligations Arising from Unjustified Enrichment

162. The Civil Code provides certain facts involving unjustified enrichment. These are cases when a benefit is obtained:

(1) through performance with no legal ground;
(2) through performance upon invalid legal ground;
(3) through performance upon a terminated legal ground;
(4) from unfair sources;
(5) through performing by another person what was to be performed by the enriched person.

(1) Unjustified Enrichment Obtained by Performance with No Legal Ground

163. The unjustified enrichment merits are characterized by the two features:

(a) there was performance, that is, property value was transferred from the property sphere of one party to the property sphere of the other party;
(b) the performance had no legal ground:

- Performance means a property benefit, presuming that somebody was provided something by it, that is, it must be of such nature that party to which performance was directed obtained a property benefit. The performance may comprise the act of giving something to somebody (a thing, money), passing on a debt and a right established or exercised in favour of somebody (e.g., a work). It may also be a performance involving an omission or a sufferance but only if the enriched party obtained a property benefit (e.g., a dwelling house owner allows another person to use it).
- Lack of legal grounds for performance may be due to the fact that from the very beginning there have been no legal grounds to perform but the performing party presumed it (performance of no-debt). Further, such cases are included here when an existing debt is performed, but in favour of someone different from the creditor, or by someone different from the debtor, or the performance is of higher value than was due from the obligation. Lack of legal ground may arise later on, too, but this case is regulated separately.

(2) Unjustified Enrichment Obtained by Performance upon an Invalid Legal Ground

164. In this case, unjustified enrichment will be established if the following prerequisites are met:

(a) Performance has been provided.
(b) The juridical act as a ground for performance is invalid:

- This prerequisite comprises similar conclusions as in the case of prerequisites of unjustified enrichment obtained through performance with no legal grounds.
- The prerequisite for successful claim to give up unjustified enrichment is the fact that the juridical act that gave the grounds for performance is invalid.

The Civil Code distinguishes voidness and voidability (see explanation on consequences of invalid juridical acts). This distinction is of significance also in the view of the right to release unjustified enrichment obtained from performance from a void or a voidable juridical act. In case of a void act, the voidness is effective from the very beginning and a subsequent extinction of the ground for voidness does not result in the validation of void juridical act. Therefore, principally every performance provided either voluntarily or due to such juridical act is an unjustified enrichment. Voidness may be claimed in fact any time with no statutory time of limitation, while the right to release performance obtained as a result of unjustified enrichment from a void juridical act will expire according to the time limitations stipulated under the Civil Code. Voidable juridical act is deemed not only existing, but also a valid juridical act by the time its voidability has been claimed. As soon as voidability has been claimed, the juridical act *ex tunc* ceases to be effective, being cancelled, and therefore the performance provided on its ground becomes an unjustified enrichment. The right to claim voidability terminates within the general three-year period of limitation. The right to claim voidability must be distinguished from the right to return performance from a voidable juridical act which becomes terminated without the limitation period stated by the Civil Code.

(3) Unjustified Enrichment Arising from a Terminated Legal Ground

165. The prerequisites for the right from unjustified enrichment to arise in this case include:

(a) Performance provided.
(b) Legal ground for performance provided has terminated:

- This prerequisite comprises similar conclusions as in the case of prerequisites of unjustified enrichment obtained through performance with no legal grounds.
- The grounds for the right to arise is the fact that the legal ground for performance provided has terminated. These are the situations where at the time of performance there existed valid legal grounds, but these legal grounds became ineffective as a result of an incurring subsequent legal event and thus terminated. It will be so, for example, when a valid withdrawal from a contract occurred for reasons stipulated under law, or under the contract, or when the withdrawal occurred by operation of law when the termination of obligation occurred as a result of the debtor's default in fixed contracts due to impossibility to perform, upon the parties' agreement or by satisfying a resolutive condition. These also may be the cases when performance is provided on the basis of an effective judgment which was subsequently revoked, for example, as a result of a new court trial. On the other hand, where a legal ground existed but terminated prior to performance (e.g., a debt was fulfilled that had become extinct by preclusion, the performance was provided only after the other party effectively

has withdrawn from the contract) this will be a performance lacking legal ground, not a performance upon a legal ground later terminated.

The benefit of unjustified enrichment obtained from performance upon legal grounds that later terminated will be involved only when the legal ground for performance had been valid. The distinction given is of significance, besides others also in the view of expiration of the right to release the unjustified enrichment.[32]

(4) Unjustified Enrichment Obtained from Unfair Sources

166. Unfair source for obtaining a property benefit can be deemed first of all in such a manner of obtaining property values that is inconsistent with good morals and as such prohibited by law. These are mainly the cases when property benefit is obtained through criminal acts, but also the cases when certain conduct cannot be criminally sanctioned for some reasons (lack of criminal liability as a result minority or incapacity of the offender).

In an overall assessment of the sources of unfairness, the presumption of fair property benefit applies. Therefore, the party claiming the giving up of property benefit on this ground must prove the source of the unfairness.

(5) Unjustified Enrichment Obtained by Another Person's Performance What Was to Be Performed by the Enriched Person

167. For the obligation to arise, the following prerequisites must be satisfied:

(a) An existing legal obligation to perform by the party instead of which it was performed.
(b) Performing the legal obligation by the party who was not due to perform:

- Unjustified enrichment in this case (contrary to the previous case) does not lie in increasing the property of the unjustly enriched person but in the fact that his assets have got rid of the liabilities as a result of his own obligation being performed by another person. Therefore, the legal duty to perform of the owing party is an indispensable prerequisite for the right under the Civil Code. This obligation may be implied in law, in a contract or in another legal situation.
- Another prerequisite is that the party in fact performing has no legal obligation to do so. Therefore, the cases when a surety performs to the creditor under the Civil Code are not included here as the surety's duty arises from the surety obligation.

32. If the performance of the seller has become impossible, his duty is discharged pursuant to §575, para. 1, Civil Code. The price sale paid by the buyer is then considered unjust enrichment resulting from performance the legal reason of which subsequently disappeared (ruling 1 Cdo 169/1996).

The same principle applied gives the basis for other Civil Code regulations the landlord's right to demand from the tenant compensation of the costs incurred by small repairs and flat maintenance that were not provided by the tenant himself and thus carried out by the tenant on his cost. In this case, as well as in others, when some rights are specifically stipulated, the special regulation applies that is of significance, namely, in the view of the prerequisites to arise.

III. Legal Consequences of Unjustified Enrichment

168. A basic legal consequence of unjustified enrichment is a rise of obligation to release this enrichment.[33] The law specifically stipulates settlement of an invalid or cancelled contract between the parties by expressing a synallagmatic nature of this obligation relationship arisen from unjustified enrichment. In this view the Civil Code should be referred to, which reflects the nature of the obligation involved also into the sphere of statutory bar.

Duty to release unjustified enrichment is owed principally by the party who obtained it. Therefore, it is the party whose assets have increased at the cost of another or the party whose assets got rid of liabilities upon performance of the obligation by the aggrieved party. If it is a natural person who is due to release unjustified enrichment, the duty mentioned is passed upon his death on his heirs, but with restrictions under the Civil Code (i.e., only up to the amount of the inherited estate).

The party entitled to demand the giving up of the unjustified enrichment is principally the one at whose expense the unjustified enrichment was obtained. Also the right to demand the giving up of unjustified enrichment is passed on to the natural person's heirs as these are not property rights restricted to the person of creditor.

Claims from unjustified enrichment may also be assigned to another person pursuant to §524 and subsequent provisions of the Civil Code.[34]

In some cases, the duty arises to give up unjustified enrichment to a person different from the one at the cost of which it was obtained. If the party at whose expense unjustified enrichment was obtained cannot be found, the enrichment must be given up to the state. The right of the state is an independent right different from the right of this party (which is of significance also in the view of statutory bar of the right of the state stated).

The duty to give up unjustified enrichment is based on the principle of the full natural restitution. The Civil Code stipulates that everything that was obtained through an unjustified enrichment must be given up. Only if it is not quite possible, especially because the enrichment involved acts, monetary compensation must be provided. The expression 'especially', used in law, allows for a broader interpretation of the prerequisite, when it is not 'quite possible' to release what was unjustifiably obtained and this is not restricted merely to the cases when performance comprised acts. In considering whether releasing and returning unjustified enrichment is 'quite possible' both subjective and objective aspects must be taken into account, as well as the economic aspects and

33. The right to have advance money from the sale price reimbursed, if the sale contract has not been made, is right from unjustified enrichment (R 27/2000).
34. *See* ruling 1 Cdo 73/2000.

all consequences of natural restitution of both of the party owing and of the party entitled.

For the extent of duty to release unjustified enrichment decisive is the moment when it was obtained. Therefore it is of no significance if in the meantime, before claiming the right to unjustified enrichment release, its value decreased or was consumed, destroyed or passed over to another person. The state before obtaining unjustified enrichment is to be reinstated through monetary compensation. Thus, the provisions of the Civil Code should be interpreted in relation with regard to the value of the unjustified enrichment obtained.

If the party that had obtained unjustified enrichment did not act bona fide, he is bound to release also the benefit obtained from it. Therefore it should be concluded from the stipulation mentioned that the duty to release involves only the duty to release benefit in fact obtained, not such that might have been, but was not obtained. Lack of bona fide is not presumed, but it must be proved by the party claiming the release of benefits on this ground.

There is an important provision of the Civil Code constituting the right of the owing party to recovery of the necessary costs incurred on the thing he releases to the party entitled. This right pertains to this party regardless of whether he acted bona fide or not when obtaining unjustified enrichment. It may only be recovery of costs usefully incurred that objectively added value to the thing and these costs were necessary or indispensable for keeping the substance or function of the thing.

The bona fide principle is further significant in the view of securing debt satisfying of the party entitled on unjustified enrichment release. Under the stipulation quoted, if the person obtaining unjustified enrichment did not act bona fide, the court may rule that the right to unjustified enrichment release may be satisfied also from the things he obtained from unjustified enrichment, including the instances when they are not subject to judgment enforcement (execution) under the Civil Procedure rules. The provision stated applies only if the duty to release unjustified enrichment is realized by monetary compensation, that is, when it is impossible to release what was unjustifiably obtained *in natura*.

Imposing the duty to release unjustified enrichment therefore aims at reparations, that is, remedy for economically and legally unfounded property transfers and restoration of the impaired principle of equivalent performance. Thus the institute of unjustified enrichment by its specific nature contributes to protection of ownership rights as well as of other property rights of natural or legal persons.

§2. Agency Without Mandate (Negotiorum Gestio)

169. An agency without a mandate is procurement of another person's matter without the procurer having a mandate or any other authorization to act. The consequences differ depending on whether the agent without mandate was averting a pending damage or whether he procured another matter.

The significant elements are procurement of a matter, the matter being another person's matter, lack of mandate or other authorization, and acting for another's benefit.

The agency is based on the premise that other person's matter may be interfered with only if he consents to it, or if it is allowed by law.

Interference in another person's matter (principal) is allowed by law only in case of pending damage; in other instances the person who wishes to procure other person's matter must inform him and wait for his consent.

Fundamental rights and obligations:

(a) in averting a pending danger the person whose matter has been procured (principal) is bound to reimburse the necessary costs to the agent even though the agent was not responsible for failure of the result;
(b) in other instances if the agent acted without a mandate he is entitled to the recovery of costs by which the person, in the interest of which the agent acted, eventually benefited.

If an agent is not entitled to reimbursement of the costs incurred, he is entitled to take, if possible, what he has procured at his cost. The agent is obliged to conclude the act, to render an account report and to hand over all that he has obtained to the person for whom he has procured the matter.

If an agent interferes in another person's matter otherwise than in averting pending damage, he is liable for the damage occurred and within this he is also liable for accidents, unless it occurred without his interference. An agent is equally liable if he interferes in another person's matters against his express will.

Selected Bibliography

Hurdík, J., P. Lavický & I. Telec. Občanské právo hmotné. Obecná část. Ochrana osobnosti. [Substantive Civil Law. General Part. Protection of Personality]. Bratislava: Poradca podnikatela, spol. s r.o., 2008.
Jakubovič, D. Záväzkové právo v intenciach českej a slovenskej komercionalistiky [Contract Law in Intentions of the Czech and Slovak Commercial Law Studies]. EPOS, 2006.
K návrhu slovenského Občianskeho zákonníka [Towards the Draft of the New Slovak Civil Code]. V. Lubyho právnické dni. Zost. Ján Lazar. Bratislava: Vyd. oddelenie PF UK, 1999.
Lazar, J. a kolektív – Občianske právo hmotné, druhé doplnené vydanie [Substantive Civil Law, 2nd revised edn]. Edícia učebníc IURA EDITION, r. 2006.
Návrh legislatívneho zámeru kodifikácie súkromného práva [Draft of the legislative intention of codification of private law]. Bratislava, 2008.
Suchoža, J. a kolektív – Obchodný zákonník, Komentár [Commercial Code, Commentary]. Bratislava: Eurounion, 2007.
Suchoža, J. & J. Husár. a kolektív – Obchodné právo [Commercial Law]. Bratislava: IURA EDITION, 2009.
Svoboda, J. a kol. – Občiansky zákonník [Civil Code]. Páté vydání. Bratislava: Eurounion, 2004.
Tóthová, M. & M. Machalcová. Protection of Consumers in Respect of Distant Contracts – Harmonization of the Theory and Practice with the Requirements of the EC/EU in the Slovak Republic. In Notitiae Ex Academia Bratislavensi Iurisprudentiae, no. 2, 2008, 185–205.
Zmluvný a zodpovednostný system v súkromnom práve [System of Contract and Liability in Private Law]. III. Lubyho právnické dni. Zost. Jozef Prusák, Bratislava: Vyd. oddelenie PF UK, 1995.
Zuklínová, M., Smlouva [Contract]. Praha: Academia, 1985.

Selected Bibliography

Index

The numbers here refer to paragraph numbers.

Index

Index

Made in the USA
Monee, IL
16 September 2026

63296747R00103